Readings in Literary Criticism 14

CRITICS ON EMILY DICKINSON

Readings in Literary Criticism

CRITICS ON EMILY DICKINSON

Readings in Literary Criticism
Edited by Richard H. Rupp

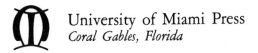

University of Miami Press
Coral Gables, Florida

CONTENTS

ACKNOWLEDGMENTS

Thomas Bailey Aldrich: from *The Atlantic Monthly,* vol. 69, 1892. Copyright © 1892 by *The Atlantic Monthly.* Reprinted by permission of the publisher.

Charles Anderson: from *Emily Dickinson's Poetry: Stairway of Surprise.* Copyright © 1960 by Charles Anderson. Reprinted by permission of Holt, Rinehart and Winston.

Louise Bogan: from "A Mystical Poet" in *Emily Dickinson: Three Views.* Copyright © 1960 by Amherst College Press. Reprinted by permission of Amherst College.

Cleanth Brooks and Robert Penn Warren: from *Understanding Poetry.* Copyright 1938 by Holt, Rinehart and Winston, Inc.: copyright © 1966 by the authors. Reprinted by permission of the publisher.

Richard Chase: from *Emily Dickinson.* Copyright 1951 by William Sloane Associates, Inc. Reprinted by permission of William Morrow and Company, Inc.

John Cody, M. D.: from *The Psychiatric Quarterly,* vol. 41, 1967. Copyright © 1967 by *The Psychiatric Quarterly.* Reprinted by permission of the author and the publisher.

Hart Crane: from *The Complete Poems and Selected Letters and Prose of Hart Crane.* Copyright 1933, 1958, 1966 by Liveright Publishers, New York. Reprinted by permission of the publisher.

J. V. Cunningham: from *The Southern Review,* vol. 5 (n.s.), 1969. Copyright © 1969 by J. V. Cunningham. Reprinted by permission of the author.

Albert Gelpi: from *Emily Dickinson: The Mind of the Poet.* Copyright 1965 by the President and Fellows of Harvard College. Reprinted by permission of Harvard University Press.

Nancy Lenz Harvey: from *The Explicator,* vol. 28, item 17. Copyright © 1970 by *The Explicator.* Reprinted by permission of the author and the publisher.

Sister Mary Humiliata: from *College English,* vol. 12, 1950. Copyright © 1950 by the National Council of Teachers of English. Reprinted by permission of the author and the publisher.

Thomas H. Johnson: from *Emily Dickinson: An Interpretive Biography.* Copyright 1955 by the President and Fellows of Harvard College. Reprinted by permission of The Belknap Press of Harvard University Press.

Jay Leyda: from *The Years and Hours of Emily Dickinson,* Vol. II. Copyright © 1960 by Yale University Press. Reprinted by permission of the publisher.

Archibald MacLeish: from "The Private World" in *Emily Dickinson: Three Views.* Copyright © 1960 by Amherst College Press. Reprinted by permission of Amherst College.

Marianne Moore: from *Collected Poems.* Copyright 1935 by Marianne Moore, 1963 by Marianne Moore and T. S. Eliot. Reprinted by permission of the Macmillan Company.

John Pickard: from *Emily Dickinson: An Introduction and Interpretation.* Copyright © 1967 by Holt, Rinehart and Winston, Inc. Reprinted by permission of the publisher.

David Porter: from *The Art of Emily Dickinson's Poetry.* Copyright 1966 by the President and Fellows of Harvard College. Reprinted by permission of Harvard University Press.

John Crowe Ransom: from "Emily Dickinson: A Poet Restored," *Perspectives USA*, no. 15, 1956. Copyright © 1956 by John Crowe Ransom. Reprinted by permission of the author.

Adrienne Rich: from *Emily Dickinson: The Mind of the Poet*. Copyright 1965 by the President and Fellows of Harvard College. Reprinted by permission of Harvard University Press.

William Rossky: from *The Explicator*, vol. 22, item 3. Copyright © 1964 by *The Explicator*. Reprinted by permission of the author and the publisher.

Ernest Sandeen: from *The New England Quarterly*, vol. 40, 1967. Copyright © 1967 by *The New England Quarterly*. Reprinted by permission of the author and the publisher.

Brita Seyersted: from *The Voice of the Poet*. Copyright 1968 by Brita Seyersted. Reprinted by permission of Harvard University Press.

Allen Tate: from "Reactionary Essays on Poetry and Ideas," in *Essays of Four Decades*. Copyright © 1969 by The Swallow Press, Chicago. Reprinted by permission of the publisher.

Hyatt H. Waggoner: from "The Transcendent Self," *Criticism*, vol. 7, 1965. Copyright © 1965 by Wayne State University Press. Reprinted by permission of the publisher.

Theodora Ward: from *The Capsule of the Mind*. Copyright 1961 by the President and Fellows of Harvard College. Reprinted by permission of The Belknap Press of Harvard University Press.

Henry W. Wells: from *Introduction to Emily Dickinson*. Copyright © 1947 by Packard and Company. Reprinted by permission of Hendricks House, Inc.

Richard Wilbur: from "Sumptuous Destitution," in *Emily Dickinson: Three Views*. Copyright © 1960 by Amherst College Press. Reprinted by permission of Amherst College.

Suzanne M. Wilson: from *American Literature*, vol. 35, 1963. Copyright © 1963 by Duke University Press. Reprinted by permission of the publisher.

Dickinson's poetry: from *The Poems of Emily Dickinson*, edited by Thomas H. Johnson. Copyright 1951, 1955 by the President and Fellows of Harvard College. Reprinted by permission of The Belknap Press of Harvard University Press and the Trustees of Amherst College.

INTRODUCTION

CRITICAL INTEREST in Emily Dickinson is a phenomenon of the twentieth century. Practically unpublished during her lifetime, the 1775 poems (whose very total was unknown until 1955) have attracted a wide critical following in recent years. Interest in her poetic contemporaries—Longfellow, Emerson, Whitman, and Melville—is growing modestly at present, but none of them has attracted the volume and quality of critical attention that Emily Dickinson has. Since 1955, when Thomas Johnson published his variorum edition of her poems, she has become in effect a new poet, a poet in our time. Only Gerard Manley Hopkins, another recluse with a posthumous reputation (and a poet with whom she has much in common) has inspired the same kind of devotion.

Indeed, devotion to Emily Dickinson is the problem. Frequently the poetry has served as a launch pad for speculative missiles aimed at her secret life. Recently critics have begun to see the poetry as autonomous, and this is all to the good. At the same time, a balanced interest in her life is legitimate and useful. The first section of this anthology is devoted to her life and death as viewed by a poet and an archivist. Hart Crane had a lifelong love for Emily Dickinson. Jay Leyda has gathered many documents surrounding her life and death: the last of them are reprinted here.

Section two represents some partial views, in both senses of the word. We may smile at Thomas Bailey Aldrich's dismissal of her work, but he reminds us of the great shift in poetic feeling which began in 1912. David Porter points out the importance of renunciation in her early poetry. In a gorgeous essay, Richard Wilbur concurs, but sees renunciation as the result of a three-fold deprivation: religion, sexual love, and reputation were denied her, and she gradually made poetry out of her pain. Allen Tate and John Crowe Ransom, two of the finest poets and critics of our time, analyze the poetic and personal sources of her work. Albert Gelpi sees her as an Apollonian, heir to Edward Taylor and ancestor of Eliot and Stevens. Thomas H. Johnson, her editor and biographer, prefers to see her as a poet of the four last things—death, judgment, heaven, and hell. Archibald MacLeish responds to his fellow poet by reading her for tone, the emotional coloring that makes her poems great. J. V. Cunningham, poet, critic, and teacher, meditates on spiritual death in Dickinson's poetry. Louise Bogan, another poet, finds analogies between mysticism and Emily's poetic vision. But before we accept Emily Dickinson as a mystic, we would do well to consider Sister Mary Humiliata's words on the subject. Clearly Emily Dickinson is no Teresa of Avila or John of the Cross, but perhaps her mysticism is a homegrown, garden variety. Finally, Suzanne M. Wilson demonstrates the values of structural analysis to the study of Emily Dickinson.

In section three of this anthology we come to the poem itself. Nancy L. Harvey explicates "What Soft Cherubic Creatures." Cleanth Brooks and Robert Penn Warren, who revolutionized the classroom teaching of poetry with their text *Understanding Poetry* in 1938, analyze "After great pain, a formal feeling comes." Their analysis is a good example of the New Critical method. Charles Anderson wrote the first full study of Emily Dickinson's poetry in 1960: he sees her poetry falling into thematic categories of art, nature, the self, and immortality. Thomas Johnson examines a poem from his special perspective as editor and biographer, while Ernest Sandeen does a thematic analysis of the late-summer poems. Brita Seyersted, like Archibald MacLeish, addresses herself to tone and poetic voice, approaching a single poem from the dual aspects of prosody and linguistics. William Rossky finds "A Clock stopped" even grimmer than we supposed. John Cody, M. D., brings the perspective of modern psychiatry to a reading of "The Soul has Bandaged moments." These six widely varying approaches suggest a few of the ways in which Emily Dickinson can be read.

Section four is a summing up. Henry Wells concludes that the use of the exact word is the cornerstone of her greatness. Richard Chase finds her center in the conflict between experience and the selves one assumes. For Theodora Ward, Emily Dickinson steered between faith and skepticism, committed only to life, and so committed to the end. Hyatt H. Waggoner discusses the problem of faith and Emily's dialogue with her father and with Emerson on the subject. John Pickard sees her as a religious poet who dwelt on the circumference of things, while Charles Anderson sees her as a religious poet who had the negative capability of the genuine artist. Adrienne Rich, finally, pays her a poetic tribute in a tone of praising wonder that Emily Dickinson would have recognized as her own.

Here then is a brief sampling of contemporary thinking about our greatest woman poet. The bibliography will suggest further reading. The whole is designed to bring the reader back, first and last, to the indispensable sources, the poems themselves. Some 75 or 100 of those poems will move, puzzle, and delight readers of this time and of time to come, so long as poems matter.

University of Miami, 1971   RICHARD H. RUPP

TABLE OF IMPORTANT DATES

1830	December 10, Emily Elizabeth Dickinson born in Amherst, Mass.
1840	Emily and her sister Lavinia enroll at Amherst Academy.
1845	Abiah Root begins a correspondence with Emily.
1846	Emily's health compels her withdrawal from Amherst Academy; she spends the summer in Boston. December, Emily resumes her studies at Amherst Academy.
1847	Emily enters Mt. Holyoke Female Seminary for one year.
1853	Death of her first mentor, B. F. Newton, in Worcester.
1855	Emily and her family go to Washington (January) for Edward Dickinson's last session in the 33rd Congress. Emily and Lavinia visit Philadelphia (March), where they hear Charles Wadsworth preach. The family moves back into the Dickinson homestead on Main Street (November); Mrs. Dickinson's long illness begins.
1856	Austin Dickinson, Emily's only brother, marries her girlhood friend Susan Gilbert and moves in next door.
1857	Ralph Waldo Emerson lectures in Amherst and visits the Austin Dickinsons.
1858	Earliest known drafts of letters to "Master." Emily begins a correspondence with Samuel Bowles.
1859	Emily begins a systematic filing of fair copy verses.
1860	Charles Wadsworth visits the Dickinson home.
1862	Emily's first letter to Thomas Wentworth Higginson (April 15). Charles Wadsworth and his family sail for San Francisco (May).
1864	Emily moves to Boston (April) for eye treatment and stays until November 28.
1865	Emily returns to Boston (April) for further treatment by Dr. Williams; she returns to Amherst in October and begins her long, gradual withdrawal from society.
1874	June 16, Edward Dickinson dies in Boston.
1875	June 15, Mrs. Edward Dickinson is paralyzed.
1880	Charles Wadsworth's last visit to Emily (August).
1881	Judge Otis P. Lord visits the Dickinsons; his visits continue until his death.
1882	April 1, Charles Wadsworth dies in Philadelphia. November 14, Mrs. Edward Dickinson dies.
1884	March 14, Judge Lord dies. June 14, first attack of Emily's final illness.
1886	May 15, Emily Dickinson dies.

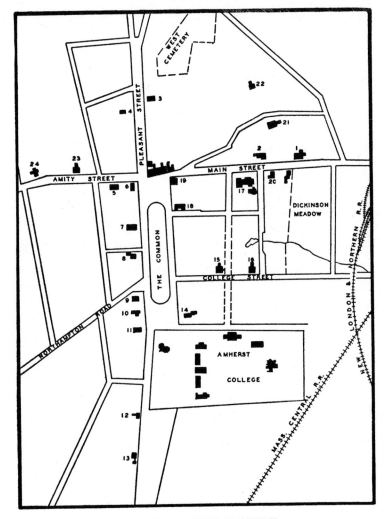

THE TOWN CENTER OF AMHERST

Redrawn from an atlas published in 1873

1. Emily Dickinson's birthplace and home, 1830-1840, 1855-1886.
2. William Austin Dickinson's house, built 1856.
3. Emily Dickinson's home, 1840-1855.
4. The Primary School.
5. Amherst Academy, 1814-1861.
6. Boltwood's Tavern, later the Amherst House.
7. The Baptist Church.
8. The "First President's House": Prof. W.C. Fowler.
9. The Meeting House, later College Hall.
10. Morgan Library (Amherst College).
11. The President's House.
12. Birthplace of Helen M. Fiske (Helen Hunt Jackson).

13. President Edward Hitchcock's house.
14. Lucius Boltwood's house.
15. Dr. Laurens P. Hickok's house.
16. President Julius H. Seelye's house.
17. The Village Church and Parsonage.
18. Grace Church (Episcopal).
19. The Town Hall.
20. Professor Richard H. Mather's house.
21. Deacon Luke Sweetser's house.
22. Professor William S. Tyler's house.
23. Professor Aaron Warner's house
24. William Cutler's house, where Susan Gilbert lived.

From George F. Whicher, *This Was A Poet* (New York: Charles Scribner's Sons, 1938), p. 150.

Life and Death

HART CRANE

To Emily Dickinson

You who desired so much—in vain to ask—
Yet fed your hunger like an endless task,
Dared dignify the labor, bless the quest—
Achieved that stillness ultimately best,

Being, of all, least sought for: Emily, hear!
O sweet, dead Silencer, most suddenly clear
When singing that Eternity possessed
And plundered momently in every breast;

—Truly no flower yet withers in your hand,
The harvest you descried and understand
Needs more than wit to gather, love to bind.
Some reconcilement of remotest mind—

Leaves Ormus rubyless, and Ophir chill.
Else tears heap all within one clay-cold hill.

(1927)

From *The Complete Poems and Selected Letters and Prose of Hart Crane,* ed.
Brom Weber (Garden City, N.Y.: Anchor Books, 1966), p. 170.

JAY LEYDA

Years and Hours of Emily Dickinson

Mrs. Todd's diary: Note *[from Austin Dickinson]* early—only "a little nearer the great event." . . . Vinnie's at 12:20. All hope given up, of course. *[After 5:00]* to Vinnie's. Emily just leaving. A few very sad minutes there . . . choir rehearsal. Across at 8:45. Emily died about six. A sad, sad *near* hour. To bed before ten, full of grief.

MAY 16. *Helen Jameson writes to her brother Frank:* Emily Dickinson died Sat. night at 5.30, of paralysis brought on by Bright's disease. What poor Vinnie will do I don't know. She seems very calm so far. Austin is much shaken.

Mrs. Todd writes to her parents: But all spirit in anything is for the time lost to me, for Emily Dickinson died last night, & everything is grey & ashen this morning. I hope you will write to Vinnie, for she is well-nigh broken-hearted & utterly bereft. Those two sisters were everything to each other, & how Vinnie will ever survive it I cannot see.

NORTHAMPTON, MAY 17. *In the Northampton* Daily Herald:
   Miss Emily Dickinson sister of W. A. Dickinson Esq., died at her brother's home on Saturday evening at six. Miss Dickinson had for many years lived a retired life. She was supposed by many of her friends to have been the author of the Saxe Holme stories . . . though she denied the fact during her life. Mrs. Helen Hunt Jackson, to whom the authorship of them has also been assigned said that she did not write them. The two were intimate friends in early life and it is possible that the stories were the joint work of each, so that each could with truth deny that she had written them.

SPRINGFIELD, MAY 18. *In the* Republican: *(Died)* At Amherst 15th, *Emily E. Dickinson,* daughter of the late Edward Dickinson.

On the editorial page, an unsigned obituary [written by Susan Dickinson]:
MISS EMILY DICKINSON OF AMHERST.
   The death of Miss Emily Dickinson, daughter of the late Edward Dickinson, at Amherst on Saturday, makes another sad inroad on the small circle so long occupying the old family mansion. It was for a long generation overlooked by death, and one passing in and out there thought of old-fashioned times, when parents and children grew up and passed maturity together, in lives of singular uneventfulness unmarked by sad or joyous crises. Very few in the village,

except among the older inhabitants, knew Miss Emily personally, although the facts of her seclusion and her intellectual brilliancy were familiar Amherst traditions. There are many houses among all classes into which her treasures of fruit and flowers and ambrosial dishes for the sick and well were constantly sent, that will forever miss those evidences of her unselfish consideration, and mourn afresh that she screened herself from close acquaintance. As she passed on in life, her sensitive nature shrank from much personal contact with the world, and more and more turned to her own large wealth of individual resources for companionship, sitting thenceforth, as some one said of her, "in the light of her own fire." Not disappointed with the world, not an invalid until within the past two years, not from any lack of sympathy, not because she was insufficient for any mental work or social career—her endowments being so exceptional—but the "mesh of her soul," as Browning calls the body, was too rare, and the sacred quiet of her own home proved the fit atmosphere for her worth and work. All that must be inviolate. . . .

Her talk and her writings were like no one's else, and although she never published a line, now and then some enthusiastic literary friend would turn love to larceny, and cause a few verses surreptitiously obtained to be printed. Thus, and through other natural ways, many saw and admired her verses, and in consequence frequently notable persons paid her visits, hoping to overcome the protest of her own nature and gain a promise of occasional contributions at least, to various magazines. She withstood even the fascinations of Mrs. Helen Jackson, who earnestly sought her co-operation in a novel of the No Name series, although one little poem somehow strayed into the volume of verses which appeared in that series. . . . A Damascus blade gleaming and glancing in the sun was her wit. Her swift poetic rapture was like the long glistening note of a bird one hears in the June woods at high noon, but can never see. Like a magician she caught the shadowy apparitions of her brain and tossed them in startling picturesqueness to her friends, who charmed with their simplicity and homeliness as well as profundity, fretted that she had so easily made palpable the tantalizing fancies forever eluding their bungling, fettered grasp. So intimate and passionate was her love of Nature, she seemed herself a part of the high March sky, the summer day and bird-call. Keen and eclectic in her literary tastes, she sifted libraries to Shakespeare and Browning; quick as the electric spark in her intuitions and analyses, she seized the kernel instantly, almost impatient of the fewest words, by which she must make her revelation. To her life was rich, and all aglow with God and immortality. With no creed, no formulated faith, hardly knowing the names of dogmas, she walked this life with the gentleness and reverence of old saints, with the firm step of martyrs who sing while they suffer. How better note the flight of this "soul of fire in a shell of pearl" than by her own words—

> Morns like these, we parted;
> Noons like these, she rose;
> Fluttering first, then firmer,
> To her fair repose.

ED's death is recorded by the Amherst town clerk:
                    Occupation: At Home.

MAY 19, WEDNESDAY. *Austin Dickinson files "Return of a Death":*
    3. Sex, and whether single, Married, or Widowed, *never married*

0. F. Bigelow files a "Physician's Certificate":
    Disease or Cause of Death,—Bright's Disease
    Duration of Sickness—2 ½ years

Austin Dickinson's diary: A little dull and hazy in the morning but grew gradually brighter—and the afternoon was all sunny and warm. At four oclock after a brief and simple service—we walked across the fields to the Cemetery.

Mrs. Todd's diary:
    Just after dinner my dear Mr. Dickinson came in with his hands full of apple-blossoms to tell me his final arrangements for the afternoon . . . At 2:30 David came & we went across to Emily's funeral. The most deliciously brilliant sunny afternoon. Simple "services"—Col. Higginson read Emily Bronte's poem on Immortality. Then we all walked quietly across the sunny fields, full of innocents & buttercups to the cemetery—

Mrs. Todd to her mother, May 23:
    The funeral—if so ghastly a name could apply to anything so poetical as the service of last Wednesday afternoon—was the most beautiful thing I ever saw. Several clergymen were there, & Col. Higginson came up from Cambridge to read Emily Bronte's poem on Immortality. The few words that he spoke to preface his reading were simply exquisite. Then President Seelye, Dr. Hitchcock & the other honorary pall-bearers took out the dainty, white casket into the sunshine, where it was lifted by the stout arms of six or eight Irish workmen, all of whom have worked about the place or been servants in the family for years, & all of whom Emily saw & talked with, occasionally, up to the last. They carried her through the fields, full of buttercups, while the friends who chose, followed on irregularly through the ferny footpaths to the little cemetery.

T. W. Higginson's diary:
    To Amherst to the funeral of that rare & strange creature Emily Dickinson. The country exquisite, day perfect, & an atmosphere of its own, fine & strange about the whole house & grounds—a more saintly & elevated "House of Usher." The grass of the lawn full of buttercups violet & wild geranium; in house a handful of pansies & another of lilies of valley on piano. E.D.'s face a wondrous restoration of youth—she is 54 [55] & looked 30, not a gray hair or wrinkle, & perfect peace on the beautiful brow. There was a little bunch of violets at the neck & one pink cypripedium; the sister Vinnie put in two

heliotropes by her hand "to take to Judge Lord." I read a poem by Emily Bronte. How large a portion of the people who have interested me have passed away.

Ellery Strickland to Martha D. Bianchi, Sept. 24, 1930: How well I remember all . . . the passing *[of ED]* to join the others . . . Then the cortege, across the lawn, through the hedge, across the fields, borne, on a special bier, by the faithful workmen of the grounds, Dennis Scannell, Steve Sullivan, Pat Ward, . . . Dennis Cashman, Dan Moynihan, Tom Kelly.

Mrs. Eudocia Flynt's diary (entry of June 8): Emily Dickinson's funeral observed, private, no flowers, taken to the Cemetery—by Irishmen, out of the back door, across the fields!! her request—

Hampshire Gazette and Northampton Courier, *May 25:* The funeral of Miss Emily Dickinson was attended at the family mansion . . . Rev. Mr. Jenkins and Rev. Mr. Dickerman performed the services and Col. Higginson of Boston read a strikingly appropriate poem. The sun was shining in glory, and all the air was sweet with the perfume of blossoming trees, as the mortal part of this gifted woman was laid beside those of her parents.

Mrs. Jameson to her son Frank, May 23:

Nothing could have been lovelier than Wed. of this past week—the day of Miss Emily's funeral—The service was suited to her—unlike any other I ever attended and very beautiful—Mr. Dickerman read her favorite passage from the scriptures—on putting off the earthly and putting on immortality, Col T W Higginson read a favorite selection of Emily Bronte and prefaced his reading (which by the way was very effective) by saying that one friend who had put on immortality, but who really never seemed to have put it off—frequently read this passage to her sister—Mr Jenkins made a good prayer . . . The body was enclosed in a white casket—with violets and ground pine over it, was carried out of the *rear* door of the hall on a bier—across the fields coming out on the street in front of Proctor Grays then coming to another foot-path over to the cemetery . . . The bearers were Pres Seelye Dr Hitchcock, Dwight Hills & yr father—The people present were invited to join in the procession & Helen & I went—It was a never to be forgotten burial and seemed singularly fitting to the departed one—The grave was lined with green boughs and all the flowers of which there was a profusion were placed in the grave with her —Just after dinner Vinnie sent over word—if I would come over I might see Miss Emily—and very glad was I of the privilege—She looked more like her brother than her sister, with a wealth of auburn hair and a very spirituelle face—She was robed in white—with a bunch of violets at her throat. Vinnie said as Emily had seen me in my picture, It was right I should see her—Sue & Emily were friends from girlhood and Vinnie was perfectly satisfied that Sue should arrange everything knowing it would be done lovingly as well as taste-fully—

From *The Years and Hours of Emily Dickinson,* 2 vols (New Haven: Yale Univ. Press, 1960), II, 472-76.

THOMAS BAILEY ALDRICH

A Poet With No Grammar

THE ENGLISH critic who said of Miss Emily Dickinson that she might have become a fifth-rate poet "if she had only mastered the rudiments of grammar and gone into metrical training for about fifteen years,"—the rather candid English critic who said this somewhat overstated his case. He had, however, a fairly good case. If Miss Dickinson had undergone the austere curriculum indicated, she would, I am sure, have become an admirable lyric poet of the second magnitude. In the first volume of her poetical chaos is a little poem which needs only slight revision in the initial stanza in order to make it worthy of ranking with some of the odd swallow flights in Heine's lyrical *intermezzo*. I have ventured to desecrate this stanza by tossing a rhyme into it, as the other stanzas happened to rhyme, and here print the lyric, hoping the reader will not accuse me of overvaluing it:—

> I taste a liquor never brewed
> In vats upon the Rhine;
> No tankard ever held a draught
> Of alcohol like mine. . . .

Certainly those inns of molten blue, and that disreputable honeygatherer who got himself turned out-of-doors at the sign of the Foxglove, are very taking matters. I know of more important things that interest me less. There are three or four bits in this kind in Miss Dickinson's book; but for the most part the ideas totter and toddle, not having learned to walk. In spite of this, several of the quatrains are curiously touching, they have such a pathetic air of yearning to be poems.

It is plain that Miss Dickinson possessed an extremely unconventional and grotesque fancy. She was deeply tinged by the mysticism of Blake, and strongly influenced by the mannerism of Emerson. The very way she tied her bonnet-strings, preparatory to one of her nunlike walks in her claustral garden, must have been Emersonian. She had much fancy of a queer sort, but only, as it appears to me, intermittent flashes of imagination. I fail to detect in her work any of that profound thought which her editor professes to discover in it. The phenomenal insight, I am inclined to believe, exists only in his partiality; for whenever a woman poet is in question Mr. Higginson always puts on his rose-colored spectacles. This is being chivalrous: but the invariable result is not clear vision. That Miss Dickinson's whimsical memoranda have a certain something which, for want of a more precise name, we term *quality* is not to be denied except by the unconvertible heathen who are not worth conversion. But the incoherence and formlessness of her—I don't know how to designate them—versicles are fatal. Sydney Smith, or some other humorist, mentions a person whose bump of veneration was so inadequately developed as to permit him to damn the equator if he wanted to. This certainly established a precedent for independence; but an eccentric, dreamy, half-educated recluse in an out-of-the-way New England village (or anywhere else) cannot with impunity set at defiance the laws of gravitation and grammar. In his charming preface to Miss Dickinson's collection, Mr. Higginson insidiously remarks: "After all, when a thought takes one's breath away, a lesson on grammar seems an impertinence." But an ungrammatical thought does not, as a general thing, takes one's breath away, except in a sense the reverse of flattering. Touching this matter of mere technique Mr. Ruskin has a word to say (it appears that he said it "in his earlier and better days"), and Mr. Higginson quotes it: "No weight, nor mass, nor beauty of execution can outweigh one grain or fragment of thought." This is a proposition to which one would cordially subscribe, if it were not so intemperately stated. A suggestive commentary on Mr. Ruskin's impressive dictum is furnished by the fact that Mr. Ruskin has lately published a volume of the most tedious verse that has been printed in this century. The substance of it is weighty enough, but the workmanship lacks just that touch which distinguishes the artist from the bungler,—the touch which Mr. Ruskin seems not to have much regarded either in his later or "in his earlier and better days."

If Miss Dickinson's *disjecta membra* are poems, then Shakespeare's prolonged imposition should be exposed without further loss of time, and Lord Tennyson ought to be advised of the error of his ways before it is too late. But I do not hold the situation to be so desperate. Miss Dickinson's versicles have a queerness and a quaintness that have stirred a momentary curiosity in emotional bosoms. Oblivion lingers in the immediate neighborhood.

From "*In Re* Emily Dickinson," *Atlantic Monthly,* 69 (January 1892), 143-44.

DAVID PORTER

Renunciation in Dickinson's Early Poetry

HER ATTITUDES represent the diverse feelings through which the poet engaged her central theme. That theme is not the abstraction death or immortality or love or fame, but rather the *act* of the mind in quest of all of these. For emotional longing, the ideal is love. For the poetic faculty, the ideal is literary achievement. For the spirit's aspiration, the ideal is immortality. We may go further than this to see that Emily Dickinson is often inexplicit in identifying the particular object of aspiration. The goals tend to fuse in unelaborated imagery of journeys, of light, of marriage. Indeed, in later poems we find a free substitution of *love* and *faith* (P-491) or *wifehood* and *immortality* (P-461). What sentimentality remains may be traced in part to the convention of sensibility informing the poetry and lesser art of letter-writing in mid-nineteenth-century New England.

The fragmentation of her poetic utterances may now reveal its rationale. Emily Dickinson's essential artistry lies partly in constructing the sharp, non-discursive image, the instant's insight committed to language. For the momentary insight to be expanded to discursive magnitude is to be false to the impulse. Gay Wilson Allen finds historical sanction for this apparent fragmentation in the literary contexts of the periods before and after Emily Dickinson. Her poetic style, he concludes, "is ejaculatory, suggestive rather than completely formed, and it is perhaps in this respect most of all that she is a link between Emerson and the 'Imagists.' "[1] Beyond the historical sanction lies the poetic temper, very modern in its assumptions, that eschews false shows of oneness in a universe where discontinuity seems the only trustworthy observation and where only provisional aggregations of fragments convey meaning and protect the observer from self-destroying doubt.[2]

Emily Dickinson's habitual choice of *renunciation,* embodied everywhere in her theme, also reflects a familiar modern outlook. We find the easy achievement avoided as often in modern poetry as in modern art. In the culture from which this art springs, says Ernst Gombrich, "renunciation of gratification, nobility, and the good converge and become one."[3] But this attitude, too, has

---

1. Gay Wilson Allen, *American Prosody* (New York, 1935), p. 319.
2. Cf. Michael Polanyi, *Personal Knowledge: Towards A Post-Critical Philosophy* (Chicago, 1960), p. 200.
3. Ernst Gombrich, *Meditations on a Hobby Horse and Other Essays on the Theory of Art* (Greenwich, Conn., 1964), p. 18.

its provenance in an earlier age. Keats believed that the realm of beauty is accessible only at the price of renunciation.[4] Faust cries out:

> What comfort can the shallow world bestow?
> Renunciation!—Learn, man, to forgo!
> This is the lasting theme of themes,
> That soon or late will show its power,
> The tune that lurks in all our dreams,
> And the hoarse whisper of each hour.[5]

The psychic responses to the knowledge that love demands compromise of one's individuality, that literary achievement is accompanied by the trespassing upon one's privacy, and that spiritual immortality requires that one forego *this* life, together constitute the pervasive questing condition about which Emily Dickinson wrote. She believed one cannot steel oneself against anguish and still remain receptive to the affection of others, one cannot withdraw and yet commune, one cannot be both a private poet and a literary celebrity, nor can one embrace the real and ideal at the same time. An undated prose fragment by the poet distills to its essence this theme which is the matrix of the early poetry. She declared: "Consummation is the hurry of fools (exhiliration of fools), but Expectation the Elixir of the Gods."[6] That theme binds into a unity the work of the formative period. . . . In "Of Bronze—and Blaze" (P-290), the speaker declares her authoritative manner is derived from viewing the magnificence of nature. The aurora borealis, she says:

> Infects my simple spirit
> With Taints of Majesty—
> Till I take vaster attitudes—
> And strut upon my stem—
> Disdaining Men, and Oxygen,
> For Arrogance of them.

In "One Year ago—jots what?" (P-296), the speaker avows an inner strength unsuspected by her lover. She responds to his assertion that his is the more profound sensibility:

> You said it hurt you—most—
> Mine—was an Acorn's Breast—
> And could not know how fondness grew
> In Shaggier Vest—
> Perhaps—I could'nt—
> But, had you looked in—
> A Giant—eye to eye with you, had been—
> No Acorn then.

---

4. *The Letters of John Keats 1814-1821*, I, 185.
5. Goethe, *Faust*, pt. I, trans. Philip Wayne (Baltimore, 1961) p. 82.
6. *Letters of Emily Dickinson* (Cambridge, 1958), III, 922.

The attitude of the speaker as victor over the pain of life, the "pale Reporter, from the awful doors" of death (P-160), is the culminating aspect of this side of the speaker's orientation. She has acquired omniscience out of anguish and perception out of pain. The tone of authority is clear in the opening lines of "I'm 'wife'—I've finished that" (P-199):

> I'm "wife"—I've finished that—
> That other state—
> I'm Czar—I'm "Woman" now—
> It's safer so.

The attitude is clear from the tone of ecstatic assurance in the familiar "I taste a liquor never brewed" (P-214). It reaches one of its most forceful professions in the declaration "Me, change! Me, alter!" (P-268):

> Me, change! Me, alter!
> Then I will, when on the Everlasting Hill
> A Smaller Purple grows—
> At sunset, or a lesser glow
> Flickers upon Cordillera—
> At Day's superior close!

"The poet's soul," John Crowe Ransom says, "... must be severe in proportion as the profuse sensibility... tends to dissipate and paralyze its force."[7] The frugal economy of the soul is, of course, apparent in this speaker who possesses enormous strength and emotional discipline. These qualities derive from the experiences of anguish, which the speaker confronts. The anguish can repeatedly be related to the condition of separation from the consummate state of mutual love, of poetic achievement, and of spiritual fulfillment. The authoritative qualities derive, indeed, from her triumph over adversity. Emily Dickinson begins a poem of 1862 (P-451) with this quatrain.

> The Outer—from the Inner
> Derives it's Magnitude—
> 'Tis Duke, or Dwarf, according
> As is the Central Mood—

In specific early poems such as "A Mien to move a Queen" and "Of Bronze—and Blaze," both of these qualities of the speaker's character are present. Yet Emily Dickinson's early capabilities are not so confined as this persistent duality suggests, but extended to burlesque, satire, and narrative. The essential duality of her speaker, however, gives us directly and most appropriately the poet's central thematic concern with aspiration. In this quest her speaker both suffers the pain of denial and develops a discipline of the emotions

---

7. John Crowe Ransom, "Emily Dickinson," *Perspectives USA*, No. 15 (Spring 1956), p. 20.

which prevents psychic disintegration. A concomitant of the quest is the visionary achievement of the goal, and in this condition the speaker flaunts her triumphant attitude.

The polarity in both theme and speaker in the early works creates tension which contributes significantly to the effectiveness of the poetry. This effectiveness is artfully enhanced by the poems' characteristic activity as performance, which in turn results from the intimate presence of the speaker. The impact of experience, both real and imagined, on her persona is defined not by the intellect, as in characteristic poetry of the Metaphysicals (with whom Emily Dickinson is somewhat wrongfully compared), but rather by the emotions. Her astonishing control in the early poems over this intense emotional activity is perhaps the most distinguishing mark of her mature artistry in the formative period.

From *The Art of Emily Dickinson's Early Poetry* (Cambridge: Harvard Univ. Press, 1966), pp. 38-39, 52-54.

ALLEN TATE

The Poetic Tradition

PERSONAL REVELATION of the kind that Donne and Miss Dickinson strove for, in the effort to understand their relation to the world, is a feature of all great poetry; it is probably the hidden motive for writing. It is the effort of the individual to live apart from a cultural tradition that no longer sustains him. But this culture, which I now wish to discuss a little, is indispensable: there is a great deal of shallow nonsense in modern criticism which holds that poetry—and this is a half-truth that is worse than false—is essentially revolutionary. It is only indirectly revolutionary: the intellectual and religious background of an age no longer contains the whole spirit, and the poet proceeds to examine that background in terms of immediate experience. But the background is necessary: otherwise all the arts (not only poetry) would have to rise in a vacuum. Poetry does not dispense with tradition; it probes the deficiencies of a tradition. But it must have a tradition to probe. It is too bad that Arnold did not explain his doctrine, that poetry is a criticism of life, from the viewpoint of its background: we should have been spared an era of academic misconception, in which criticism of life meant a diluted pragmatism, the criterion of which was respectability. The poet in the true sense "criticizes" his tradition, either as such, or indirectly by comparing it with something that is about to replace it; he does what the root-meaning of the verb implies—he *discerns* its real elements and thus establishes its value, by putting it to the test of experience.

What is the nature of a poet's culture? Or, to put the question properly, what is the meaning of culture for poetry? All the great poets become the material of what we popularly call culture: we study them to acquire it. It is clear that Addison was more cultivated than Shakespeare; nevertheless Shakespeare is a finer source of culture than Addison. What is the meaning of this? Plainly it is that learning has never had anything to do with culture except instrumentally: the poet must be exactly literate enough to write down fully and precisely what he has to say, but no more. The source of a poet's true culture lies back of the paraphernalia of culture, and not all the historical activity of an enlightened age can create it.

A culture cannot be consciously created. It is an available source of ideas that are imbedded in a complete and homogeneous society. The poet finds himself balanced upon the moment when such a world is about to fall, when it threatens to run out into looser and less self-sufficient impulses. This world order is assimilated, in Miss Dickinson, as medievalism was in Shakespeare, to the poetic vision; it is brought down from abstraction to personal sensibility.

In this connection it may be said that the prior conditions for great poetry, given a great talent, may be reduced to two: the thoroughness of the poet's discipline in an objective system of truth, and his lack of consciousness of such a discipline. For this discipline is a number of fundamental ideas the origin of which the poet does not know; they give form and stability to his fresh perceptions of the world; and he cannot shake them off. This is his culture, and, like Tennyson's God, it is nearer than hands and feet. With reasonable certainty we unearth the elements of Shakespeare's culture, and yet it is equally certain—so innocent was he of his own resources—that he would not know what our discussion is about. He appeared at the collapse of the medieval system as a rigid pattern of life, but that pattern remained in Shakespeare what Shelley called a "fixed point of reference" for his sensibility. Miss Dickinson, as we have seen, was born into the equilibrium of an old and a new order. Puritanism could not be to her what it had been to the generation of Cotton Mather—a body of absolute truths: it was an unconscious discipline timed to the pulse of her life.

The perfect literary situation: it produces, because it is rare, a special and perhaps the most distinguished kind of poet. I am not trying to invent a new critical category. Such poets are never very much alike on the surface; they show us all the varieties of poetic feeling; and, like other poets, they resist all classification but that of temporary convenience. But, I believe, Miss Dickinson and John Donne would have this in common: their sense of the natural world is not blunted by a too-rigid system of ideas: yet the ideas, the abstractions, their education or their intellectual heritage, are not so weak as to let their immersion in nature, or their purely personal quality, get out of control. The two poles of the mind are not separately visible; we infer them from the lucid tension that may be most readily illustrated by polar activity. There is no thought as such at all: nor is there feeling: there is that unique focus of experience which is at once neither and both.

Like Miss Dickinson, Shakespeare is without opinions: his peculiar merit is also deeply involved in his failure to think about anything; his meaning is not in the content of his expression: it is in the tension of the dramatic relations of his characters. This kind of poetry is at the opposite of intellectualism. (Miss Dickinson is obscure and difficult, but that is not intellectualism.) To T. W. Higginson, the editor of *The Atlantic Monthly,* who tried to advise her, she wrote that she had no education. In any sense that Higginson could understand, it was quite true. His kind of education was the conscious cultivation of abstractions. She did not reason about the world she saw: she merely saw it. The "ideas" implicit in the world within her rose up, concentrated in her immediate perception.

That kind of world at present has for us something of the fascination of a buried city. There is none like it. When such worlds exist, when such cultures flourish, they support not only the poet but all members of society. For, from these, the poet differs only in his gift for exhibiting the structure, the internal lineaments, of his culture by threatening to tear them apart: a process that concentrates the symbolic emotions of society while it seems to attack them. The poet may hate his age; he may be an outcast like Villon; but this world is always there as the background to what he has to say. It is the lens through which he brings nature to focus and control—the clarifying medium that concentrates his personal feeling. It is ready-made; he cannot make it; with it, his poetry has a spontaneity and a certainty of direction that, without it, it would lack. No poet could have invented the ideas of "The Chariot," only a great poet could have found their imaginative equivalents. Miss Dickinson was a deep mind writing from a deep culture, and when she came to poetry, she came infallibly.

Infallibly, at her best; for no poet has ever been perfect, nor is Emily Dickinson. Her precision of statement is due to the directness with which the abstract framework of her thought acts upon its unorganized material. The two elements of her style, considered as point of view, are immortality, or the idea of permanence, and the physical process of death or decay. Her diction has two corresponding features: words of Latin or Greek origin and, sharply opposed to these, the concrete Saxon element. It is this verbal conflict that gives her verse its high tension; it is not a device deliberately seized upon, but a feeling for language that senses out the two fundamental components of English and their metaphysical relation: the Latin for ideas and the Saxon for perceptions— the peculiar virtue of English as a poetic language.

Like most poets Miss Dickinson often writes out of habit: the style that emerged from some deep exploration of an idea is carried on as verbal habit when she has nothing to say. She indulges herself:

> There's something quieter than sleep
> Within this inner room!
> It wears a sprig upon its breast,
> And will not tell its name.
>
> Some touch it and some kiss it,
> Some chafe its idle hand:
> It has a simple gravity
> I do not understand!
>
> While simple hearted neighbors
> Chat of the "early dead,"
> We, prone to periphrasis,
> Remark that birds have fled!

It is only a pert remark; at best a superior kind of punning—one of the worst specimens of her occasional interest in herself. But she never had the slightest interest in the public. Were four poems or five published in her lifetime? She never felt the temptation to round off a poem for public exhibition.

Higginson's kindly offer to make her verse "correct" was an invitation to throw her work into the public ring—the ring of Lowell and Longfellow. He could not see that he was tampering with one of the rarest literary integrities of all time. Here was a poet who had no use for the supports of authorship—flattery and fame; she never needed money.

She had all the elements of a culture that has broken up, a culture that on the religious side takes its place in the museum of spiritual antiquities. Puritanism, as a unified version of the world, is dead; only a remnant of it in trade may be said to survive. In the history of puritanism she comes between Hawthorne and Emerson. She has Hawthorne's matter, which a too irresponsible personality tends to dilute into a form like Emerson's; she is often betrayed by words. But she is not the poet of personal sentiment; she has more to say than she can put down in any one poem. Like Hardy and Whitman, she must be read entire; like Shakespeare, she never gives up her meaning in a single line.

She is therefore a perfect subject for the kind of criticism which is chiefly concerned with general ideas. She exhibits one of the permanent relations between personality and objective truth, and she deserves the special attention of our time, which lacks that kind of truth.

She has Hawthorne's intellectual toughness, a hard, definite sense of the physical world. The highest flights to God, the most extravagant metaphors of the strange and the remote, come back to a point of casuistry, to a moral dilemma of the experienced world. There is, in spite of the homiletic vein of utterance, no abstract speculation, nor is there a message to society; she speaks wholly to the individual experience. She offers to the unimaginative no riot of vicarious sensation; she has no useful maxims for men of action. Up to this point her resemblance to Emerson is slight: poetry is a sufficient form of utterance, and her devotion to it is pure. But in Emily Dickinson the puritan world is no longer self-contained; it is no longer complete; her sensibility exceeds its dimensions. She has trimmed down its supernatural proportions; it has become a morality; instead of the tragedy of the spirit there is a commentary upon it. Her poetry is a magnificent personal confession, blasphemous and, in its self-revelation, its honesty, almost obscene. It comes out of an intellectual life toward which it feels no moral responsibility. Cotton Mather would have burnt her for a witch.

From "Emily Dickinson," in *Reactionary Essays on Poetry and Ideas* (1959); rpt. in *Emily Dickinson: A Collection of Critical Essays,* ed. Richard B. Sewell (Englewood Cliffs, N.J.: Prentice-Hall, 1963), pp. 16-27.

ALBERT GELPI

Emily As Apollonian

DESPITE HER indebtedness to Emerson, Emily Dickinson's verse is not Emersonian. Like Schiller's sentimental poet and unlike Emerson's artist in "The Snow-Storm," she knew that art had more to do than merely mimic the "frolic architecture" of Nature. When it came to specific matters of approach and technique, when it came to writing a poem and practicing her craft, she did not belong to the prophetic or Dionysian strain of American poetry which derived palely from Emerson and descended lustily through Whitman to Carl Sandburg and Jeffers, and more recently to Jack Kerouac and Brother Antoninus. If for the moment's convenience American poetry may be divided broadly into opposing tendencies, the deliberate and formalistic quality of Dickinson's verse associates her rather with the diverse yet Apollonian tradition which proceeds from Edward Taylor through her to Eliot, Stevens, Frost, and Marianne Moore, and thence to Robert Lowell and Elizabeth Bishop. The dynamic energies of Whitman's language open out to shatter the form and "stand witness to a world beyond the world of his making."[1] No matter what Emily Dickinson might say about the poet's vatic function, the dynamic energies of her language close tightly to assert the presence of an aesthetic object of the poet's making.

A good indication of her formalism is her insatiable and unabating interest in the wiles of words (again one thinks of Marianne Moore).[2] Emily told Higginson that for some years her lexicon had been her only companion, and throughout her life she pored over the dictionary as zealously as she read her Bible. From the native strength of words and from her experiments in expanding their scope she fashioned a unique language (Higginson thought it "spasmodic" and "uncontrolled."[3]) She chose words with stinging freshness; she flavored speech with earthy New England colloquialisms; she often dropped

---

1. "A Conversation With Brother Antoninus," *The Harvard Advocate,* 97 (Spring 1963), 39.
2. See Miss Moore's "To a Snail":

> If 'compression is the first grace of style,'
> you have it. Contractility is a virtue
> as modesty is a virtue.
> . . . .
> in the absence of feet, 'a method of conclusion';
> 'a knowledge of principles',
> in the curious phenomenon of your occipital horn.

3. L II 409.

the "s" of the third-person singular of the present tense to suggest the enduring quality of the action; she emphasized nouns by the striking addition or omission of the preceding article; she sometimes used singular nouns where plurals were expected and vice versa; she made parts of speech perform unorthodox functions, used words in startling contexts, coined words when none seemed available or apt.[4] Like Ezra Pound, William Carlos Williams, Marianne Moore, and E.E. Cummings, Emily Dickinson sought to speak the uniqueness of her experience in a personal tongue by reconstituting and revitalizing—at the risk of eccentricity—the basic verbal unit.

From *Emily Dickinson: The Mind of the Poet* (Cambridge: Harvard Univ. Press, 1965), pp. 146-47.

4. For experiments with words, see, for example: "The Seldoms of the Mind" (L II 509); "Water grows," "That Caspian Fact," "Sahara dies" (P1291 III 896); "Zero at the bone" (P986 II 712); "Summer's circumspect" (P1298 III 901); "Death's Immediately" (P1420 III 985); "Intro without my Trans" (P1530 III 1055); "Meek my Vive le roi" (P151 I 108); "Marine Walk" (L III 858); "a Must," "a Shall" (P1618 III 1110); "On their Passage Cashmere" (P86 I 70); "The Transitive of Bells" (P633 II 486-487); "among Circumference" (P798 II 604); "ablative to show" (P1744 III 1172). For coined words, see, for example: birdling (P39 I 33); swang (P42 I 35); o'ertakeless (P282 I 201); goer by (P283 I 202); New Englandly (P285 I 204); optizan (P329 I 263); crucifixal (P364 I 289); hostiler (P705 II 542); undivine (P751 II 572); consciouser (P762 II 580); vitalless (P770 II 584); perceiveless (P843 II 637); mis sum (P877 II 651); kinsmansless (P1019 II 729): antiquest (P1068 II 752); exody (P1300 III 905); redoubtablest (P1417 III 983); graphicer (P1422 III 986); overtakelessness (P1691 III 1147).

JOHN CROWE RANSOM

Dickinson's Poetic Personality

IT IS the love poems which are decisive for the literary personality of Emily Dickinson. Most probably the poems would not have amounted to much if the author had not finally had her own romance, enabling her to fulfill herself like any other woman. She always had quick and warm affections for people, and she loved nature spontaneously with what Wordsworth might almost have called a passion. But here are the love poems, with their erotic strain. Now it happens that the god was in this instance again a blind god, or perhaps we should allow also for the possibility that the style of the romance fitted exactly into a secret intention of her own—at any rate it still appears to be the fact, for Mr. Johnson confirms it, that her grand attachment was directed to the person of a blameless clergyman who was already married. She could never have him. We know next to nothing as to what passed between them, for his letters to her have all been destroyed, except apparently for one letter, pastoral but friendly in its tone. And what becomes of the experience asserted so decently yet passionately in the poems? That was all imaginary, says Mr. Johnson roundly, if I follow him; and does not even add that it was necessary to the effectiveness of the poems. It would seem very likely that he is right about the fact; it is so much "in character," insofar as we are able to understand herself and her situation. Mr. Johnson is himself a native and a historian of her region, the valley of the Connecticut at Amherst, where in her time the life and the metaphysics were still in the old Puritan tradition, being almost boastfully remote from what went on across the state in Boston. In her Protestant community the gentle spinsters had their assured and useful place in the family circle, they had what was virtually a vocation. In a Roman community they might have taken the veil. But Emily Dickinson elected a third vocation, which was the vocation of poet. And the point is that we cannot say she deviated in life from her honest status of spinster, and did not remain true to the vows of this estate, so to speak, as did the innumerable company of her sisters. But it was otherwise for the literary personality which she now projected.

We can put this most topically nowadays, perhaps, if we say that about 1861, when Emily Dickinson had come into her thirties, she assumed in all serious-ness her vocation of poet and therefore, and also, what William Butler Yeats would have called her poet's mask: the personality which was antithetical to her natural character and identical with her desire. By nature gentle but indecisive, plain in looks, almost anonymous in her want of any memorable history, she chose as an artist to claim a heroic history which exhibited first a great passion, then renunciation and honor, and a passage into the high experiences of a purified Soul. That is the way it would seem to figure out. And we have an interesting literary parallel if we think in these terms about the poetry of her contemporary, Walt Whitman. A good deal of notice has been paid lately to Whitman by way of pointing out that he was an impostor, because the aggressive masculinity which he asserted so blatantly in the poems was only assumed. But that would be Walt Whitman's mask. Whitman and Emily Dickinson were surely the greatest forces of American poetry in the nineteenth century, and both had found their proper masks. (Poe would be the third force, I think; just as original, but not a poetic force that was at the same time a moral force.)

But in Emily Dickinson's own time and place she could not but be regarded as an unusually ineffective instance of the weaker sex. She was a spinster, becoming more and more confirmed in that character. And not a useful spinster, but a recluse, refusing to enter into the world. Next, an eccentric; keeping to her room, absenting herself even from household and kitchen affairs. Perhaps a sort of poet, but what of that? The town of Amherst knew she could make verses for Saint Valentine's Day, and was always ready to send somebody a poem to accompany a flower, or a poem to turn a compliment or a condolence; once in a long while it was known that a poem got into print; but it scarcely mattered. It is a great joke now, though not at her expense, to discover with Mr. Johnson that the poems sent out on these occasions were often from her finest store.

The slighting of the professional poet in her life-time is made up for in our time by especial gallantries on her behalf and an exquisite hatred for those who neglected her. Perhaps the most satisfying image of her, from this perspective, would now see Emily Dickinson as a kind of Cinderella, in a variant version of the story with a different moral. The original story surely sprang from man's complacent image of woman. The Ur-Cinderella scrubbed away at her pots and pans and never stopped until the kind Prince came by and took her away to his palace, where virtue had its reward. Our own Cinderella could do without the Prince; she preferred her clergyman, and he did not take her anywhere. She proceeded to take her own self upstairs, where she lived, happy ever after with her memories, her images, and her metaphysics.

She busied herself with writing, revising, and sometimes fabulously perfecting those slight but intense pieces; for the eye of the future. When there were enough of them she would stitch them down the sides together into a packet, like a little book, and put it into the cherry bureau drawer. We may suppose that she did not fail to wonder sometimes, in that ironical wisdom which steadied and protected her: What if her little packets might never catch the great public eye? But this was not her responsibility.

Among her most literate acquaintances it is scarcely possible that there was one (or more than one, says Mr. Johnson) who would not have told her, had it not been too cruel, that if she was clever enough to know the accomplishments it took to make a real poet, she would be clever enough to know better than try to be one. Consider her disabilities. She had a good school education which gave her some Latin, but after a year in Miss Lyon's advanced school for young ladies at Mount Holyoke she did not return, and we cannot quite resolve the ambiguity of whether this was due to her wish or to her poor health. She read well but not widely; the literature which gave her most was the hymnbook. And she was amazed when she was asked why she did not travel; was there not enough of the world where she was already? When she made her decision to be a poet, it is true that she sent som poems to a man of letters and wanted to know if she should continue. The gentleman answered kindly, and entered into a lifelong correspondence with her, but did not fail to put matters on a proper footing by giving her early to understand that she might as well not seek to publish her verse. And she made little effort to find another counsellor. Perhaps it seemed to her that there was no particular correlation between being a poet and having the literary companionship of one's peers.

Of course all her disabilities worked to her advantage. Let us have a look at that hymnbook. She had at hand, to be specific, a household book which was well known in her period and culture, Watts' *Christian Psalmody,* (Her father's copy is still to be seen.) In it are named, and illustrated with the musical notations, the Common Meter, the Long, the Short, and a dozen variations which had been meticulously carried out in the church music of her New England. Her own poems used these forms with great accuracy, unless sometimes she chose to set up variations of her own, or to relax and loosen the rules. Since she was perfect in her command of these meters, they gave her a formal mastery over the substantive passion of the verse. But since these meters excluded all others, their effect was limiting. Her meters are all based upon Folk Line, the popular form of verse, and the oldest in our language. I have been used to saying that the great classics of this meter are the English Ballads and Mother Goose, both very fine, and certainly finer than most of the derivative verse done by our poets since the middle of the eighteenth century. Hereafter I must remember to add another to these classics: the Protestant hymnbooks, but especially the poetry of Emily Dickinson, which is their derivative. Folk Line is disadvantageous if it is used on the wrong poetic occasion, or if it denies to the poet the use of English Pentameter when that would be more suitable. Pentameter is the staple of what we may call the studied or "university" poetry, and it is capable of containing and formalizing many kinds of substantive content which would be too complex for Folk Line. Emily Dickinson appears never to have tried it.

The final disability which I have to mention, and which for me is the most moving, has been most emphatically confirmed in Mr. Johnson's book. Her sensibility was so acute that it made her excessively vulnerable to personal contacts. Intense feeling would rush out as soon as sensibility apprehended the object, and flood her consciousness to the point of helplessness. When visitors called upon the family, she might address them from an inner door and then hide herself; but if deep affection was involved she was likely to send word that she must be excused altogether, and post a charming note of apology later. She kept up her relations with many friends, but they were conducted more and more by correspondence; and in that informal genre she was of the best performers of the century. The happy encounter was as painful as the grievous one. But we need not distress ourselves too sorely over this disability when we observe the sequel. It made her practice a kind of art on all the social occasions; conducting herself beautifully though rather theatrically in the oral exchanges, and writing her notes in language styled and rhythmed remarkably like her poetry.

It was even better than that. The poet's Soul, she might have said, must have its housekeeping, its economy, and that must be severe in proportion as the profuse sensibility, which is the poet's primary gift, tends to dissipate and paralyze its force; till nothing remains but a kind of exclamatory gaping. The Soul must learn frugality, that is, how to do with a little of the world, and make the most of it; how to concentrate, and focus, and come remorseless and speedy to the point. That is a kind of renunciation; all good poets are familiar with it. And critics, too, I believe. Do we not all profess a faith in the kind of art which looks coolly upon the turgid deliverance of sensibility and disciplines it into beauty?

From "Emily Dickinson: A Poet Restored," *Perspectives USA,* No. 15 (Spring 1956); rpt. in *Emily Dickinson: A Collection of Critical Essays,* ed. Richard B. Sewell (Englewood Cliffs, N.J.: Prentice-Hall, 1963), pp. 88-100.

THOMAS H. JOHNSON

Emily As Eschatologist

DEALING with her final theme, the love of God, Emily Dickinson went
beyond theological orthodoxy. One observes how she felt that eternity is tied
into love now, yesterday, and always. All immortality for her was a quality of
spirit, a vital force, to be recognized in this life. She wrote Samuel Bowles,
whose integrity she felt matched his zest for living: "You have the most
triumphant face out of Paradise, probably because you are there constantly,
instead of ultimately"; and after his death in 1878 she phrased the thought
again to Mary Bowles: "As he was himself Eden, he is with Eden, for we cannot
become what we were not." This sense of intimacy with the everlasting she
strikingly expressed again to Mary Bowles two years later: "Immortality as a
guest is sacred, but when it becomes as with you and with us, a member of
the family, the tie is more vivid." She is thinking of the fact that both her father
and "Mr. Sam" are dead and, she likes to think, enjoying paradise together,
but she is signifying her belief that immortality, as all love must, begins at
home. It is, she says, a way of life that can be elected. "Paradise is of the
option," she once wrote Colonel Higginson. "Whosoever will—own Eden
notwithstanding Adam and Repeal." She carried the thought forward with a
penetration which her friends among the clergy must have found exhilarating,
even though they could not theologically have supported it. In her letter of
condolence to Colonel Higginson after the death of his wife Mary Channing
Higginson, she said: "To be human is more than to be divine, for when Christ
was divine, he was uncontented till he had been human."

She has gone beyond all Christian orthodoxies by conferring upon the
creature a partnership with the Creator. She insists that love is meaningless
unless it is reciprocated, both in this life and in the life to come; and that God
himself is not yet perfected, and perhaps never will be. Man of course is totally
dependent upon God, but in some way, to some degree, God needs the love
of man to keep the cycles wheeling and the stars in their course. To this extent
Jehovah for her is not Zeus, all-sufficient, infallible, and arbitrary; but Prometheus, the friend of mankind, capable of suffering. She has also in mind the
love which St. Paul talks about as the possession of all men who search their
own hearts to find it: "Love is it's own rescue," she continues in her letter to
Higginson, "for we—at our supremest, are but it's trembling Emblems." "My
Faith is larger than the Hills," she declares, because it endures beyond the
phenomena of nature.

> So when the Hills decay—
> My Faith must take the Purple Wheel
> To show the Sun the way—"

And she concludes:

> How dare I, therefore, stint a faith
> On which so vast depends—
> Lest Firmament should fail for me—
> The Rivet in the Bands.

This concept of man as the rivet, whose love thereby allows God to achieve fulfillment, suggests a four-dimensional concept of the universe wherein all elements are interdependent. It throws clear light upon the nature of her skepticism. To have less faith in the upward striving creature than in the outstretched arm of the Creator, she says here and often elsewhere, is to expect a less than perfect union between God and man. Viewed in this light, her query many years later "Is immortality true?" was only a way of asking whether the theological concept of an arbitrary and self-sufficient deity did in fact get at the whole truth.

> As plan for Noon and plan for Night
> So differ Life and Death
> In positive Prospective—
> The Foot upon the Earth
>
> At Distance, and Achievement, strains,
> The Foot upon the Grave
> Makes effort at conclusion
> Assisted faint of Love.

The same ringing assurance appears in such poems as "Faith—is the Pierless Bridge," "I never saw a moor," and "Split the Lark—and you'll find the Music"—the last with its taunt at those who would classify the unknowable:

> Scarlet Experiment! Sceptic Thomas!
> Now, do you doubt that your Bird was true?

There is Promethean rebelliousness in such poems as "Bind me—I still can sing." The will to share burns insistently in a large number of the poems written during this cycle.

> So large my Will
> The little that I may
> Embarrasses
> Like gentle infamy—
>
> Affront to Him
> For whom the Whole were small
> Affront to me
> Who know His Meed of all.

> Earth at the best
> Is but a scanty Toy—
> Bought, carried Home
> To Immortality.
>
> It looks so small
> We chiefly wonder then
> At our Conceit
> In purchasing.

. . . .

In "Behind Me—dips Eternity" she conceives of herself as "the Term between" it and the immortality ahead. Here death is:

> . . . but the Drift of Eastern Gray,
> Dissolving into Dawn away,
> Before the West begin—

Her profoundest insights focus in the poem "The Admirations—and Contempts of Time," which she says, "Show justest—through an Open Tomb." The fact of dying "Reorganizes Estimate," so that we have, as it were,

> Compound Vision—
> Light—enabling Light—
> The Finite—furnished
> With the Infinite—
> Convex—and Concave Witness—
> Back—toward Time—
> And forward—
> Toward the God of Him—

Love, faith, death, immortality—the four dimensions—are the forces by which the willing creature is bound to the willing God. Her currents here flow into all subterranean oceans. The search for the meaning of love could take her this far in 1864:

> Till Death—is narrow Loving—
> The Scantest Heart extant
> Will hold you till your privilege
> Of Finiteness—be spent—
>
> But He whose loss procures you
> Such Destitution that
> Your Life too abject for itself
> Thenceforward imitate—
>
> Until—Resemblance perfect—
> Yourself, for His pursuit

Delight of Nature—abdicate—
Exhibit Love—somewhat—

Love goes infinitely beyond the grave, and we become better images of those we loved because we try to imitate them. Thus are we made willing to die.

Unable are the Loved to die
For Love is Immortality
Nay, it is Deity

Her muse has led her to the discovery of secret springs in her own desert.

The skilful portraiture of aspects of nature lie ahead; a thunderstorm, sunset, or pebble; a cricket, hummingbird, or oriole. Some of them are among the first order of nature lyrics, and they typify the deepened sympathies now rechanneled for the most part into her voluminous correspondence. They were written during the last fifteen years of her life when her outward activities, so far as they could be observed by neighbors, seemed confined to caring for her invalid mother, tending her flowers, and enjoying the association of small children. The few friends who knew her well were aware of the inner activity which never abated. But her philosophic testament had been written by 1865. Her first interest, "circumference," would be her last. In 1864 she could express her sense of immortality with classic restraint:

Ample make this Bed
Make this Bed with Awe
In it wait till Judgment break
Excellent and Fair

Be it's Mattrass straight
Be it's Pillow round
Let no Sunrise' Yellow noise
Interrupt this Ground.

Twenty years later, ill and measuring the weeks of her own distance from awe and circumference, she could write this stave:

Back from the cordial Grave I drag thee
He shall not take thy Hand
Nor put his spacious arm around thee
That none can understand

Prometheus to the last, she wishes to participate with amplitude in the limits that are universal.

From *Emily Dickinson: An Interpretive Biography,* (Cambridge: The Belknap Press of Harvard Univ. Press), 1955, pp. 254-59.

ARCHIBALD MACLEISH

The Private World

NO ONE can read these poems . . . without perceiving that he is not so much reading as being spoken to. There is a curious energy in the words and a tone like no other most of us have ever heard. Indeed, it is the tone rather than the words that one remembers afterwards. Which is why one comes to a poem of Emily's one has never read before as to an old friend.

But what then is the tone? How does this unforgettable voice speak to us? For one thing, and most obviously, it is a wholly spontaneous tone. There is no literary assumption of posture or pose in advance. There is no sense that a subject has been chosen—that a theme is about to be developed. Occasionally, in the nature pieces, the sunset scenes, which are so numerous in the early poems, one feels the presence of the pad of water-color paper and the mixing of the tints, but when she began to write as poet, which she did, miraculously, within a few months of her beginnings as a writer, all that awkwardness disappears. Breath is drawn and there are words that will not leave you time to watch her coming toward you. Poem after poem—more than a hundred and fifty of them—begins with the word "I," the talker's word. She is already in the poem before she begins it, as a child is already in the adventure before he finds a word to speak of it. To put it in other terms, few poets and they among the most valued—Donne comes again to mind—have written more *dramatically* than Emily Dickinson, more in the live locutions of dramatic speech, words born living on the tongue, written as though spoken. It is almost impossible to begin one of her successful poems without finishing it. The punctuation may bewilder you. The density of the thing said may defeat your understanding. But you will read on nevertheless because you will not be able to stop. Something is being *said* to *you* and you have no choice but hear.

And this is a second characteristic of the voice—that it not only speaks but speaks to *you*. We are accustomed in our time—unhappily accustomed, I think—to the poetry of the overheard soliloquy, the poetry written by the poet to himself or to a little group of the likeminded who can be counted on in advance to "understand." Poetry of this kind can create universes when the poet is Rilke but even in Rilke there is something sealed and unventilated about the creation which sooner or later stifles the birds. The subject of poetry is the human experience and its object must therefore be humanity even in a time like ours when humanity seems to prefer to limit its knowledge of the experience of life to the life the advertisers offer it. It is no excuse to a poet that humanity will not listen. It never has listened unless it was made to—and least of all, perhaps, in those two decades of the Civil War and after in which Emily Dickinson wrote.

The materialism and vulgarity of those years were not as flagrant as the materialism and vulgarity in which we live but the indifference was greater. America was immeasurably farther from Paris, and Amherst was incomparably farther from the rest of America, and in and near Amherst there were less than a dozen people to whom Emily felt she could show her poems—and only certain poems at that. But her poems, notwithstanding, were never written to herself. The voice is never a voice over-heard. It is a voice that speaks to us almost a hundred years later with such an urgency, such an immediacy, that most of us are half in love with this girl we call by her first name, and read with scorn Colonel Higginson's description of her as a "plain, shy little person . . . without a single good feature." We prefer to remember her own voice describing her eyes—"like the sherry the guest leaves in the glass."

There is nothing more paradoxical in the whole history of poetry, to my way of thinking, than Emily Dickinson's commitment of that live voice to a private box full of pages and snippets tied together with little loops of thread. Other poets have published to the general world poems capable of speaking only to themselves or to one or two beside. Emily locked away in a chest a voice which cries to all of us of our common life and love and death and fear and wonder.

Or rather, does *not* cry. For that is a third characteristic of this unforgettable tone: that it does not clamor at us even when its words are the words of passion or of agony. This is a New England voice—it belongs to a woman who "sees New Englandly"—and it has that New England restraint which is really a self-respect which also respects others. There is a poem of Emily's which none of us can read unmoved—which moves me, I confess, so deeply that I cannot always read it. It is a poem which, in another voice, might indeed have cried aloud, but in hers is quiet. I think it is the quietness which moves me most. It begins with these six lines:

> I can wade Grief—
> Whole Pools of it—
> I'm used to that—
> But the least push of Joy
> Breaks up my feet—
> And I tip—drunken (252)

One has only to consider what this might have been, written otherwise by another hand—for it would have had to be another hand. Why is it not maudlin with self-pity here? Why does it truly touch the heart and the more the more it is read? Because it is impersonal? It could scarcely be more personal. Because it is oblique?—Ironic? It is as candid as agony itself. No, because there IS no self-pity. Because the tone which can contain "But the least push of Joy / Breaks up my feet" is incapable of self-pity. Emily is not only the actor in this poem, she is the removed observer of the action also. When we drown in self-pity we throw ourselves into ourselves and go down. But the writer of this poem is both in it and out of it: both suffers it and sees. Which is to say that she is poet.

There is another famous poem which makes the same point:

> She bore it till the simple veins
> Traced azure on her hand—
> Till pleading, round her quiet eyes
> The purple Crayons stand.
>
> Till Daffodils had come and gone
> I cannot tell the sum,
> And then she ceased to bear it
> And with the Saints sat down.(144)

Here again, as so often in her poems of death—and death is, of course, her constant theme—the margin between mawkishness and emotion is thin, so thin that another woman, living, as she lived, in constant contemplation of herself, might easily have stumbled through. But here again what saves her, and saves the poem, is the tone: "She bore it till . . . " "And then she ceased to bear it—/And with the Saints sat down." If you have shaped your mouth to say "And with the Saints sat down" you cannot very well weep for yourself or for anyone else, veins purple on the hand or not.

Anyone who will read Emily's poems straight through in their chronological order in Thomas H. Johnson's magnificent Harvard edition will feel, I think, as I do, that without her extraordinary mastery of tone her achievement would have been impossible. To write constantly of death, of grief, of despair, of agony, of fear is almost to insure the failure of art, for these emotions overwhelm the mind and art must surmount experience to master it. A morbid art is an imperfect art. Poets must learn Yeats's lesson that life is tragedy but if the tragedy turns tragic for them they will be crippled poets. Like the ancient Chinese in *Lapis Lazuli,* like our own beloved Robert Frost who has looked as long and deeply into the darkness of the world as a man well can, "their eyes, their ancient glittering eyes" must be *gay.* Emily's eyes, color of the sherry the guests leave in the glass, had that light in them:

> Dust is the only Secret—
> Death, the only One
> You cannot find out all about
> In his "native town."
>
> Nobody knew "his Father"—
> Never was a Boy—
> Hadn't any playmates,
> Or "Early history"—

Industrious! Laconic!
Punctual! Sedate!
Bold as a Brigand!
Stiller than a Fleet!

Builds, like a Bird, too!
Christ robs the Nest—
Robin after Robin
Smuggled to Rest!(153)

Ezra Pound, in his translation of *The Women of Trachis,* has used a curiously
compounded colloquialism which depends on just such locutions to make the
long agony of Herakles supportable. Emily had learned the secret almost a
century before.

But it is not only agony she is able to put in a supportable light by her
mastery of tone. She can do the same thing with those two opposing subjects
which betray so many poets: herself and God. She sees herself as small and
lost and doubtless doomed—but she sees herself always, or almost always, with
a saving smile which is not entirely tender:

Two full Autumns for the Squirrel
Bounteous prepared—
Nature, Hads't thou not a Berry
For thy wandering Bird? (846)

and

I was a Phebe—nothing more—
A Phebe—nothing less—
The little note that others dropt
I fitted into place—

I dwelt too low that any seek—
Too shy, that any blame—
A Phebe makes a little print
Upon the Floors of Fame—(1009)

and

A Drunkard cannot meet a Cork
Without a Revery—
And so encountering a Fly
This January Day
Jamaicas of Remembrance stir
That send me reeling in—
The moderate drinker of Delight
Does not deserve the spring—(1628)

I suppose there was never a more delicate dancing on the crumbling edge of
the abyss of self-pity—that suicidal temptation of the lonely—than Emily's,

but she rarely tumbles in. She sees herself in the awkward stumbling attitude
and laughs.

As she laughs too, but with a child's air of innocence, at her father's Puritan God, that Neighbor over the fence of the next life in the hymnal:

> Abraham to kill him
> Was distinctly told—
> Isaac was an Urchin—
> Abraham was old—
>
> Not a hesitation—
> Abraham complied—
> Flattered by Obeisance
> Tyranny demurred—
>
> Isaac—to his children
> Lived to tell the tale—
> Moral—with a Mastiff
> Manners may prevail. (1317)

It is a little mocking sermon which would undoubtedly have shocked Edward
Dickinson with his "pure and terrible" heart, but it brings the god of Abraham
closer to New England than he had been for the two centuries preceding—
brings him, indeed, as close as the roaring lion in the yard: so close that he
can be addressed politely by that child who always walked with Emily hand in
hand:

> Lightly stepped a yellow star
> To its lofty place
> Loosed the Moon her silver hat
> From her lustral Face
> All of the Evening softly lit
> As an Astral Hall
> Father I observed to Heaven
> You are punctual—(1672)

But more important than the confiding smile which makes it possible to speak
familiarly to the God of Elder Brewster is the hot and fearless and wholly
human anger with which she is able to face him at the end. Other poets have
confronted God in anger but few have been able to manage it without rhetoric
and posture. There is something about that ultimate face to face which excites
and embarrassing self-consciousness in which the smaller of the two opponents
seems to strut and "beat it out even to the edge of doom." Not so with Emily.
She speaks with the laconic restraint appropriate to her country, which is New
England, and herself, which is a small, shy gentlewoman who has suffered
much:

Of God we ask one favor,
That we may be forgiven—
For what, he is presumed to know—
The Crime, from us, is hidden—
Immured the whole of Life
Within a magic Prison (1601)

It is a remarkable poem and its power, indeed its possibility, lies almost altogether in its voice, its tone. The figure of the magic prison is beautiful in itself, but it is effective in the poem because of the level at which the poem is spoken—the level established by that "he is presumed to know." At another level even the magic prison might well become pretentious.

But it is not my contention here that Emily Dickinson's mastery of tone is merely a negative accomplishment, a kind of lime which prepares the loam for clover. On the contrary I should like to submit that her tone is the root itself of her greatness. The source of poetry, as Emily knew more positively than most, is a particular awareness of the world. "It is that," she says, meaning by "that" a poet, which "Distills amazing sense/From ordinary Meanings," and the distillation is accomplished not by necromancy but by perception—by the particularity of the perception—which makes what is "ordinary meaning" to the ordinary, "amazing sense" to the poet. The key to the poetry of any poem, therefore, is its particularity—the uniqueness of its vision of the world it sees. In some poems the particularity can be found in the images into which the vision is translated. In others it seems to exist in the rhythm which carries the vision "alive into the heart." In still others it is found in a play of mind which breaks the light of the perception like a prism. The particularity has as many forms almost as there are poets capable of the loneliness in which uniqueness is obliged to live. With Emily Dickinson it is the tone and timbre of the speaking voice. When she first wrote Colonel Higginson to send him copies of her verses she asked him to tell her if they "breathed" and the word, like all her words, was deliberately chosen. She knew, I think, what her verses were, for she knew everything that concerned her.

I should like to test my case, if I can call it that, on a short poem of four lines written probably on the third anniversary of her father's death. It is one of her greatest poems and perhaps the only poem she ever wrote which carries the curious and solemn weight of perfection. I should like you to consider wherein this perfection lies:

Lay this Laurel on the One
Too intrinsic for Renown—
Laurel—vail your deathless tree—
Him you chasten, that is He! (1393)

From *Emily Dickinson: Three Views* (Amherst: Amherst College Press, 1960), pp. 17-26.

J. V. CUNNINGHAM

A Poet of Spiritual Catastrophe

"TITLE DIVINE is mine," she says, (1072) and certainly the title she claims is divine, "Empress of Calvary." She is the bride of Christ of suffering and Redemption. It is "Acute degree," that is, by the device of proximate word, high rank. But she is "The wife without the sign," "Royal, all but the crown." "Now *sign, seal, crown* are technical terms in the theology of Revelation. She is without "an appearance or occurrence indicative of the divine presence, and authenticating a message or messenger." And she lacks the crown of life: "Be thou faithful unto death, and I will give thee a crown of life." (Rev. 2: 10) In brief, she is self-elected. She has, in fact, become married without the ordinary accompaniments of earthly marriage:

> Betrothed without the swoon
> God sends us women when you hold
> Garnet to garnet, gold to gold.

She has been "Born, bridalled, shrouded in a day, / Tri-victory." Reborn, as depicted in other poems, by a second baptism: "except a man be born again, he cannot see the kingdom of God." (John: 3:3) She has been bridalled, and the heavenly bridal suggests the earthly:

> "My husband," women say,
> Stroking the melody.
> Is this the way?

Is this experience of mine, she asks, of the same kind as ordinary marriage? Nor is the transition surprising, for as we all know, as John Humphrey Noyes knew, "Religious love is very near neighbor to sexual love. . . . The next thing a man wants, after he has found the salvation of his soul, is to find his Eve and his Paradise," and to find them in terms of the theology of Revelation. So "There came a day at summer's full" when "Each was to each the sealed church," each was the saved and the source of salvation to the other, bound by exchange of crucifixes, which I take figuratively:

> Sufficient troth that we shall rise,
> Deposed at length the grave,
> To that new marriage justified
> Through Calvaries of love.

(322)

The marriage is new; that is, the marriages of this world are cancelled. The two are spiritual spouses "sealed to eternity" not through the mediation of the Son, but through each other's private love and suffering—a strange doctrine of Justification! We do not know what other person was involved: the name, as elsewhere in Dickinson, may be *N.* What was involved, however, is clear.

Hence in another poem she asserts, "I'm wife." (199) There is here no theological reference, and indeed no other person: "I'm wife. Stop there!" This is spiritual marriage, that curious phenomenon of nineteenth-century revivalism, in a special form, and deprived of spouse. Noyes will again instruct us as to the nature of the experience. He writes to Abagail Merwin, an early disciple and early defector:

> Let it be distinctly understood at the outset, that I intend no interference with any earthly engagement. . . . At length in the midst of another series of sufferings at Prospect I saw you again clothed in white robes, and by the word of the Lord you were given to me. . . . I know now that my love for you is the gift of God, pure and free, above all jealousy and above all fear I can say of you to my Father : "She was thine, and thou gavest her to me; all mine are thine, and thine are mine." Nothing can shake my assurance that in a coming time you will be my joy and crown "a diadem of glory from the land of the Lord."

"Born, bridalled, shrouded in a day, / Tri-victory!" The experience, I think, is simultaneous, not successive—in another poem (473) she is "Baptized this day a bride"—and the crucial element is "shrouded." Attempted conversion involves, in Dickinson it is willfully provoked by, a fantasy of dying, what Noyes calls "the consciousness of dying." The poems that issue from this spiritual exercise are among her most impressive. In one she heard a fly buzz when she died:

> and then it was
> There interposed a fly
>
> With blue, uncertain, stumbling buzz
> Between the light and me,
> And then the windows failed, and then
> I could not see to see.
>
> (465)

In another she presides at her own funeral:

> I felt a funeral in my brain,
> And mourners to and fro
> Kept treading, treading, till it seemed
> That sense was breaking through.

And when they all were seated
A service, like a drum,
Kept beating, beating, till I thought
My mind was going numb.

And then I heard them lift a box
And creak across my soul
With those same boots of lead again,
Then Space began to toll

As all the Heavens were a bell
And Being but an ear,
And I and Silence some strange race
Wrecked, solitary here.

And then a plank in reason broke
And I dropped down and down,
And hit a world at every plunge,
And finished knowing then.

                                                                    (280)

Toward the close the experience expands into that of a double divided self:
on the one hand, the total engrossment of being in the universe; on the other,
personal identity and Silence, non-being, alienated and outcast. Lost. And to
be lost is to lose all. So she passes out; it is a psychotic episode.

In other poems she gives up the enterprise, gives up hope, the preparatory
stage, and with it the fear:

When I hoped, I feared.
Since I hoped I dared.
Everywhere alone
As a church remain.

                                                                    (1181)

"As a church"? This is a peculiarly Dickinson idiom, as in "I wish I was a
hay!" Thus, to remain a church, everywhere alone, is to be one of a Church
Triumphant whose membership is one. Personal religion with a vengeance?
Or the necessity of despair?

So she can finally view the consequences with acceptance, even with spiritual
snobbery:

The missing All prevented me
From missing minor things.
If nothing larger than a world's
Departure from a hinge,
Or sun's extinction, be observed,

> 'Twas not so large that I
> Could lift my forehead from my work
> For curiosity.

(985)

Only loss of salvation justifies such hyperbole.

Some of the poems that have been cited are good, some indifferent, and some really bad, but all in the service of understanding and realization. Let us conclude, then, by bringing our inquiries to bear on a poem universally acknowledged to be of her best. We find the proximate word: the "heft / Of cathedral tunes," instead of "the weight," suggests irrelevant associations with handling instead of oppressiveness, whereas "the look of death," as earlier remarked, is exact. We find, not the fallacy of wilful fancy, but Ruskin's other pathetic fallacy, "shadows hold their breath." The odd-numbered lines vary from six to eight syllables with no significance in the variation. In kind, it is a report of a repetitive and involuntary experience, "None may teach it any"; it is not to be argued with; a nature experience yet theological in form, "heavenly hurt"; it is the intimation that one is sealed to Perdition: " 'Tis the Seal, Despair!"

> There's a certain slant of light,
> Winter afternoons,
> That oppresses like the heft
> Of cathedral tunes.
>
> Heavenly hurt it gives us;
> We can find no scar,
> But internal difference
> Where the meanings are.
>
> None may teach it any;
> 'Tis the Seal, Despair!
> An imperial affliction
> Sent us of the air.
>
> When it comes, the landscape listens,
> Shadows hold their breath;
> When it goes, 'tis like the distance
> On the look of death.

(258)

From "Sorting Out: The Case of Dickinson." *Southern Review*. NS 5 (Spring 1969), 436-56.

RICHARD WILBUR

Sumptuous Destitution

AT SOME point Emily Dickinson sent her whole Calvinist vocabulary into exile, telling it not to come back until it would subserve her own sense of things.

Of course, that is not a true story, but it is a way of saying what I find most remarkable in Emily Dickinson. She inherited a great and overbearing vocabulary which, had she used it submissively, would have forced her to express an established theology and psychology. But she would not let that vocabulary write her poems for her. There lies the real difference between a poet like Emily Dickinson and a fine versifier like Isaac Watts. To be sure, Emily Dickinson also wrote in the metres of hymnody, and paraphrased the Bible, and made her poems turn on great words like Immortality and Salvation and Election. But in her poems those great words are not merely being themselves; they have been adopted, for expressive purposes; they have been taken personally, and therefore redefined.

The poems of Emily Dickinson are a continual appeal to experience, motivated by an arrogant passion for the truth. "Truth is so rare a thing," she once said, "it is delightful to tell." And, sending some poems to Colonel Higginson, she wrote, "Excuse them, if they are untrue." And again, to the same correspondent, she observed, "Candor is the only wile"—meaning that the writer's bag of tricks need contain one trick only, the trick of being honest. That her taste for truth involved a regard for objective fact need not be argued: we have her poem on the snake, and that on the hummingbird, and they are small masterpieces of exact description. She liked accuracy; she liked solid and homely detail; and even in her most exalted poems we are surprised and reassured by buckets, shawls, or buzzing flies.

But her chief truthfulness lay in her insistence on discovering the facts of her inner experience. She was a Linnaeus to the phenomena of her own consciousness, describing and distinguishing the states and motions of her soul. The results of this "psychic reconnaissance," as Professor Whicher called it, were several. For one thing, it made her articulate about inward matters which poetry had never so sharply defined; specifically, it made her capable of writing two such lines as these:

> A perfect, paralyzing bliss
> Contented as despair.

We often assent to the shock of a paradox before we understand it, but those lines are so just and so concentrated as to explode their meaning instantly in the mind. They did not come so easily, I think, to Emily Dickinson. Unless I guess wrongly as to chronology, such lines were the fruit of long poetic research; the poet had worked toward them through much study of the way certain emotions can usurp consciousness entirely, annulling our sense of past and future, cancelling near and far, converting all time and space to a joyous or grievous here and now. It is in their ways of annihilating time and space that bliss and despair are comparable.

Which leads me to a second consequence of Emily Dickinson's self-analysis. It is one thing to assert as pious doctrine that the soul has power, with God's grace, to master circumstance. It is another thing to find out personally, as Emily Dickinson did in writing her psychological poems, that the aspect of the world is in no way constant, that the power of external things depends on our state of mind, that the soul selects its own society and may, if granted strength to do so, select a superior order and scope of consciousness which will render it finally invulnerable. She learned these things by witnessing her own courageous spirit.

Another result of Emily Dickinson's introspection was that she discovered some grounds, in the nature of her soul and its affections, for a personal conception of such ideas as Heaven and Immortality, and so managed a precarious convergence between her inner experience and her religious inheritance. What I want to attempt now is a rough sketch of the imaginative logic by which she did this. I had better say before I start that I shall often seem demonstrably wrong, because Emily Dickinson, like many poets, was consistent in her concerns but inconsistent in her attitudes. The following, therefore, is merely an opinion as to her main drift.

Emily Dickinson never lets us forget for very long that in some respects life gave her short measure; and indeed it is possible to see the greater part of her poetry as an effort to cope with her sense of privation. I think that for her there were three major privations: she was deprived of an orthodox and steady religious faith; she was deprived of love; she was deprived of literary recognition.

At the age of 17, after a series of revival meetings at Mount Holyoke Seminary, Emily Dickinson found that she must refuse to become a professing Christian. To some modern minds this may seem to have been a sensible and necessary step; and surely it was a step toward becoming such a poet as she became. But for her, no pleasure in her own integrity could then eradicate the feeling that she had betrayed a deficiency, a want of grace. In her letters to Abiah Root she tells of the enhancing effect of conversion on her fellow-students, and says of herself in a famous passage:

> *I* am one of the lingering bad ones, and so do I slink away, and pause and ponder, and ponder and pause, and do work without knowing why, not surely, for this brief world, and more sure it is not for heaven, and I ask what this message *means* that they ask for so very eagerly: *you* know of this depth and fulness, will you try to tell me about it?

There is humor in that, and stubbornness, and a bit of characteristic lurking pride: but there is also an anguished sense of having separated herself, through some dry incapacity, from spiritual community, from purpose, and from magnitude of life. As a child of evangelical Amherst, she inevitably thought of purposive, heroic life as requiring a vigorous faith. Out of such a thought she later wrote:

> The abdication of Belief
> Makes the Behavior small—
> Better an ignis fatuus
> Than no illume at all—(1551)

That hers was a species of religious personality goes without saying; but by her refusal of such ideas as original sin, redemption, hell, and election, she made it impossible for herself—as Professor Whicher observed—"to share the religious life of her generation." She became an unsteady congregation of one.

Her second privation, the privation of love, is one with which her poems and her biographies have made us exceedingly familiar, though some biographical facts remain conjectural. She had the good fortune, at least once, to bestow her heart on another; but she seems to have found her life, in great part, a history of loneliness, separation, and bereavement.

As for literary fame, some will deny that Emily Dickinson ever greatly desired it, and certainly there is evidence mostly from her latter years, to support such a view. She *did* write that "Publication is the auction/ Of the mind of man." And she *did* say to Helen Hunt Jackson, "How can you print a piece of your soul?" But earlier, in 1861, she had frankly expressed to Sue Dickinson the hope that "sometime" she might make her kinfolk proud of her. The truth is, I think, that Emily Dickinson knew she was good, and began her career with a normal appetite for recognition. I think that she later came, with some reason, to despair of being understood or properly valued, and so directed against her hopes of fame what was by then a well-developed disposition to renounce. That she wrote a good number of poems about fame supports my view: the subjects to which a poet returns are those which vex him.

What did Emily Dickinson do, as a poet, with her sense of privation? One thing she quite often did was to pose as the laureate and attorney of the empty-handed, and question God about the economy of His creation. Why, she asked, is a fatherly God so sparing of His presence? Why is there never a sign that prayers are heard? Why does Nature tell us no comforting news of its Maker? Why do some receive a whole loaf, while others must starve on a crumb? Where is the benevolence in shipwreck and earthquake? By asking such questions as these, she turned complaint into critique, and used her own sufferings as experiential evidence about the nature of the deity. The God who emerges from these poems is a God who does not answer, an unrevealed God whom one cannot confidently approach through Nature or through doctrine.

But there was another way in which Emily Dickinson dealt with her sentiment of lack—another emotional strategy which was both more frequent and
more fruitful. I refer to her repeated assertion of the paradox that privation is
more plentiful than plenty; that to renounce is to possess the more; that "The
Banquet of abstemiousness/ Defaces that of wine." We all know how the
poet illustrated this ascetic paradox in her behavior—how in her latter years
she chose to live in relative retirement, keeping the world, even in its dearest
aspects, at a physical remove. She would write her friends, telling them how
she missed them, then flee upstairs when they came to see her; afterward, she
might send a note of apology, offering the odd explanation that "We shun
because we prize." Any reader of Dickinson biographies can furnish other examples, dramatic or homely, of this prizing and shunning, this yearning and
renouncing: in my own mind's eye is a picture of Emily Dickinson watching
a gay circus caravan from the distance of her chamber window.

In her inner life, as well, she came to keep the world's images, even the
images of things passionately desired, at the remove which renunciation
makes; and her poetry at its most mature continually proclaims that to lose or
forego what we desire is somehow to gain. We may say, if we like, with some
of the poet's commentators, that this central paradox of her thought is a ra-
tionalization of her neurotic plight; but we had better add that it is also a discovery of something about the soul. Let me read you a little poem of psychological observation which, whatever its date of composition may logically be
considered as an approach to that discovery.

> Undue Significance a starving man attaches
> To Food—
> Far off—He sighs—and therefore—Hopeless—
> And therefore—Good—
>
> Partaken—it relieves—indeed—
> But proves us
> That Spices fly
> In the Receipt—It was the Distance—
> Was Savory—(439)

This poem describes an educational experience, in which a starving man is
brought to distinguish between appetite and desire. So long as he despairs of
sustenance, the man conceives it with the eye of desire as infinitely delicious.
But when, after all, he secures it and appeases his hunger, he finds that its
imagined spices have flown. The moral is plain: once an object has been mag-
nified by desire, it cannot be wholly possessed by appetite.

The poet is not concerned, in this poem, with passing any judgment. She is
simply describing the way things go in the human soul, telling us that the
frustration of appetite awakens or abets desire, and that the effect of intense
desiring is to render any finite satisfaction disappointing. Now I want to read
you another well-known poem, in which Emily Dickinson was again consid-

ering privation and possession, and the modes of enjoyment possible to each. In this case, I think, a judgment is strongly implied.

> Success is counted sweetest
> By those who ne'er succeed.
> To comprehend a nectar
> Requires sorest need.
>
> Not one of all the purple Host
> Who took the Flag today
> Can tell the definition
> So clear of Victory
>
> As he defeated—dying —
> On whose forbidden ear
> The distant strains of triumph
> Burst agonized and clear!(67)

Certainly Emily Dickinson's critics are right in calling this poem an expression of the idea of compensation—of the idea that every evil confers some balancing good, that through bitterness we learn to appreciate the sweet, that "Water is taught by thirst." The defeated and dying soldier of this poem is compensated by a greater awareness of the meaning of victory than the victors themselves can have: he can comprehend the joy of success through its polar contrast to his own despair.

The poem surely does say that; yet it seems to me that there is something further implied. On a first reading, we are much impressed with the wretchedness of the dying soldier's lot, and an improved understanding of the nature of victory may seem small compensation for defeat and death; but the more one ponders this poem the likelier it grows that Emily Dickinson is arguing the *superiority* of defeat to victory, of frustration to satisfaction, and of anguished comprehension to mere possession. What do the victors have but victory, a victory which they cannot fully savor or clearly define? They have paid for their triumph by a sacrifice of awareness; a material gain has cost them a spiritual loss. For the dying soldier, the case is reversed: defeat and death are attended by an increase of awareness, and material loss has led to spiritual gain. Emily Dickinson would think that the better bargain.

In the first of these two poems I have read, it was possible to imagine the poet as saying that a starving man's visions of food are but wish fulfillments, and hence illusory; but the second poem assures us of the contrary — assures us that food, or victory, or any other good thing is best comprehended by the eye of desire from the vantage of privation. We must now ask in what way desire can define things, what comprehension of nectars it can have beyond a sense of inaccessible sweetness.

. . . .

Here is an eight-line poem of her own, in which she comprehends the full sweetness of water.

> We thirst at first—'tis Nature's Act—
> And later—when we die—
> A little Water supplicate—
> Of fingers going by—
>
> It intimates the finer want—
> Whose adequate supply
> Is that Great Water in the West—
> Termed Immortality—(726)

Emily Dickinson elected the economy of desire, and called her privation good, rendering it positive by renunciation. And so she came to live in a huge world of delectable distances. Far-off words like "Brazil" or "Circassian" appear continually in her poems as symbols or things distanced by loss or renunciation, yet infinitely prized and yearned-for. So identified in her mind are distance and delight that, when ravished by the sight of a hummingbird in her garden, she calls it "the mail from Tunis." And not only are the objects of her desire distant; they are also very often moving away, their sweetness increasing in proportion to their remoteness. "To disappear enhances," one of the poems begins, and another closes with these lines:

> The Mountain—at a given distance—
> In Amber—lies—
> Approached—the Amber flits—a little—
> And That's—the Skies—(572)

To the eye of desire, all things are seen in a profound perspective, either moving or gesturing toward the vanishing-point. Or to use a figure which may be closer to Miss Dickinson's thought, to the eye of desire the world is a centrifuge, in which all things are straining or flying toward the occult circumference. In some such way, Emily Dickinson conceived her world, and it was in a spatial metaphor that she gave her personal definition of Heaven. "Heaven," she said, "is what I cannot reach."

At times it seems that there is nothing in her world but her own soul, with its attendant abstration, and, at a vast remove, the inscrutable Heaven. On most of what might intervene she has closed the valves of her attention, and what mortal objects she does acknowledge are riddled by desire to the point of transparency. Here is a sentence from her correspondence: "Enough is of so vast a sweetness, I suppose it never occurs, only pathetic counterfeits." The writer of that sentence could not invest her longings in any finite object. Again she wrote, "Emblem is immeasurable—that is why it is better than fulfillment, which can be drained." For such a sensibility, it was natural and necessary that things be touched with infinity. Therefore her nature poetry, when most serious, does not play descriptively with birds or flowers but presents us repeatedly with dawn, noon, and sunset, those grand ceremonial moments of the day which argue the splendor of Paradise. Or it shows us the ordinary landscape transformed by the electric brilliance of a storm; or it shows us the fields succumbing to the annual mystery of death. In her love-poems, Emily Dickinson was at first covetous of the beloved himself; indeed, she could be idolatrous, going so far as to say that his face, should she see it again in Heaven, would eclipse the face of Jesus. But in what I take to be her later work is the beloved's lineaments, which were never very distinct, vanish entirely; he becomes pure emblem, a symbol of remote spiritual joy, and so is all but absorbed into the idea of Heaven. The lost beloved is, as one poem declares, "infinite when gone," and in such lines as the following we are aware of him mainly as an instrument in the poet's commerce with the beyond.

> Of all the Souls that stand create—
> I have elected—One—
> When Sense from Spirit—files away—
> And Subterfuge—is done—
> When that which is—and that which was—
> Apart—intrinsic—stand—
> And this brief Tragedy of Flesh—
> Is shifted—like a Sand—
> When Figures show their royal Front—
> And Mists—are carved away,
> Behold the Atom—I preferred—
> To all the lists of Clay!(664)

In this extraordinary poem, the corporeal beloved is seen as if from another and immaterial existence, and in such perspective his earthly person is but an atom of clay. His risen spirit, we presume, is more imposing, but it is certainly not in focus. What the rapt and thudding lines of this poem portray is the poet's own magnificence of soul—her fidelity to desire, her confidence of Heaven, her contempt of the world. Like Cleopatra's final speeches, this poem is an irresistible demonstration of spiritual status, in which the supernatural is so royally demanded that skepticism is disarmed. A part of its effect derives, by the way, from the fact that the life to come is described in an ambiguous present tense, so that we half-suppose the speaker to be already in Heaven.

There were times when Emily Dickinson supposed this of herself, and I want to close by making a partial guess at the logic of her claims to beatitude. It seems to me that she generally saw Heaven as a kind of infinitely remote bank, in which, she hoped, her untouched felicities were drawing interest. Parting, she said, was all she knew of it. Hence it is surprising to find her saying, in some poems, that Heaven has drawn near to her, and that in her soul's "superior instants" Eternity has disclosed to her "the colossal substance/ Of immortality." Yet the contradiction can be understood, if we recall what sort of evidence was persuasive to Emily Dickinson.

"Too much of proof," she wrote, "affronts belief"; and she was little convinced either by doctrine or by theological reasoning. Her residual Calvinism was criticized and fortified by her study of her own soul in action, and from the phenomena of her soul she was capable of making the boldest inferences. That the sense of time is subject to the moods of the soul seemed to her a proof of the soul's eternity. Her intensity of grief for the dead, and her feeling of their continued presence, seemed to her arguments for the reunion of souls in Heaven. And when she found in herself infinite desires, "immortal longings," it seemed to her possible that such desires might somewhere be infinitely answered.

One psychic experience which she interpreted as beatitude was "glee," or as some would call it, euphoria. Now a notable thing about glee or euphoria is its gratuitousness. It seems to come from nowhere, and it was this apparent sourcelessness of the emotion from which Emily Dickinson made her inference. "The 'happiness' without a cause," she said, "is the best happiness, for glee intuitive and lasting is the gift of God." Having foregone all earthly causes of happiness, she could only explain her glee, when it came, as a divine gift—a compensation in joy for what she had renounced in satisfaction, and a foretaste of the mood of Heaven. The experience of glee, as she records it, is boundless: all distances collapse, and the soul expands to the very circumference of things. Here is how she put it in one of her letters: "Abroad is close tonight and I have but to lift my hands to touch the 'Hights of Abraham.' " And one of her gleeful poems begins,

> 'Tis little—I could care for Pearls—
> Who own the ample sea—

How often she felt that way we cannot know, and it hardly matters. As Robert Frost has pointed out, happiness can make up in height for what it lacks in length; and the important thing for us, as for her, is that she construed the experience as a divine gift. So also she thought of the power to write poetry, a power which, as we know, came to her often; and poetry must have been the chief source of her sense of blessedness. The poetic impulses which visited her seemed "bulletins from Immortality," and by their means she converted all her losses into gains, and all the pains of her life to that clarity and repose which were to her the qualities of Heaven. So superior did she feel, as a poet, to earthly circumstance, and so strong was her faith in words, that she more than once presumed to view this life from the vantage of the grave.

In a manner of speaking, she *was* dead. And yet her poetry, with its articulate faithfulness to inner and outer truth, its insistence on maximum consciousness, is not an avoidance of life but an eccentric mastery of it. . . .

From *Emily Dickinson: Three Views* (Amherst: Amherst College Press, 1960), pp. 35-46.

LOUISE BOGAN

A Mystical Poet

POETS DOWN the centuries, visited by that power which the ancients call *the Muse,* have described their experience in much the same way as the mystic describes his ecstatic union with Divine Truth. This experience has been rendered at length, and dramatically, by Dante, as well as by St. John of the Cross; and certain poems in the literature of every language attest to moments when, for the poet, "the deep and primal life which he shares with all creation has been roused from its sleep." And both poets and mystics have described with great poignance that sense of deprivation and that shutting away from grace which follows the loss of the vision (or of the inspiring breath), which is called, in the language of mysticism, "the dark night of the soul."

Certainly one of the triumphs brought about by the emergence of the Romantic spirit, in English poetry, at the end of the eighteenth century, was a freeing and an enlargement of poetic vision, and in the nineteenth century we come upon a multiplication of poets whose spiritual perceptions were acute. Beyond Vaughan and Herbert (who, in the seventeenth century, worked from a religious base) we think of Blake, of the young Wordsworth; of Keats and Shelley; of Emily Brontë; of Gerard Manley Hopkins; and we can extend the list into our own day with the names of Yeats and T. S. Eliot. By examining the work of these poets—to whom the imagination, the creative spirit of man, was of utmost importance—we find that the progress of the mystic toward illumination, and of the poet toward the full depth and richness of his insight—are much alike. Both work from the world of reality, toward the realm of Essence; from the microcosm to the macrocosm. Both have an intense and accurate sense of their surroundings; there is nothing vague or floating in their perception of reality; it is indeed as though they saw "through, not with, the eye." And they are filled with love for the beauty they perceive in the world of time—"this remarkable world" as Emily Dickinson called it; and concerning death they are neither fearful nor morbid—how could they be, since they feel immortality behind it? They document life's fearful limitations from which they suffer, but they do not mix self-pity with the account of their suffering (which they describe, like their joy, in close detail). They see the world in a grain of sand and Heaven in a wild flower; and now and again they bring eternity into focus, as it were, in a phrase of utmost clarity. In the work of Emily Dickinson such moments of still and halted perception are many. The slant of light on a winter day, the still brilliance of a summer noon, the sound of the wind before the rain—she speaks of these, and we share the shock of insight, the slight dislocation of serial events, the sudden shift from the Manifold into the One.

One of the dominant facts concerning Emily Dickinson is her spirit of religious unorthodoxy. Her deeply religious feeling ran outside the bounds of dogma; this individualism was, in fact, an inheritance from her Calvinist forbears, but it was out of place when contrasted to the Evangelicanism to which, in her time, so many Protestants had succumbed. She early set herself against the guilt and gloom inherent in this revivalism. She avoided the constrictions which a narrow insistence on religious rule and law would put upon her. She had read Emerson with delight, but as Yvor Winters has remarked, it is a mistake to think of her as a Transcendentalist in dimity. Here again she worked through to a standpoint and an interpretation of her own; her attitude toward pain and suffering, toward the shocking facts of existence, was far more realistic than Emerson's. As we examine her chief spiritual preoccupations, we see how closely she relates to the English Romantic poets who, a generation or so before her, fought a difficult and unpopular battle against the eighteenth century's cold logic and mechanical point of view. The names of Blake and Coleridge come to mind; we know that to both these poets the cold theory of Locke represented "a deadly heresy on the nature of existence." It is difficult to look back to this period of early Romantic breakthrough, since so much of that early boldness and originality was later dissipated in excesses of various kinds. But it is important to remember that Blake attached the greatest importance to the human imagination as an aspect of some mystery beyond the human, and to listen to his ringing words: "The world of Imagination is the world of Eternity. . . . The world of Imagination is Infinite and Eternal, whereas the world of generation is Finite and Temporal . . ."—and to remember, as well, that "Blake, Wordsworth, Coleridge, Shelley and Keats shared the belief that the imagination was nothing less than God as he operates in the human soul." C. M. Bowra, writing of the Romantic ethos in general, brings out a fact which has been generally overlooked: that, although Romantic poetry became a European phenomenon, English Romantic poetry "almost alone . . . connected visionary insight with a superior order of being." "There is hardly a trace of this (insight)," Bowra goes on to say, "in Hugo, or Heine or Lermontov. They have their full share of longing, but almost nothing of Romantic vision. . . . " Hölderlin, in Germany tried to share a lost vision of Greece, but on the whole it was the English who accomplished a transformation in thought and emotion "for which there is no parallel in their age." It is surely in the company of these English poets that Emily Dickinson belongs. At its most intense, her vision not only matched, but transcended theirs; she crossed the same boundaries with a like intransigence; and the same vigorous flowers sprang from different seeds, in the spirit of a woman born in 1830, in New England, in America.

The drawing of close parallels between the life and circumstances of poets is often an unrewarding task. But in the case of Emily Dickinson because hers was for so long considered a particularly isolated career, it is interesting to make certain comparisons. It has been pointed out that there is a close resemblance between the lives, temperament and works of Emily Brontë and Emily Dickinson. And one or two resemblances between Emily Dickinson and Blake (Blake taken as a lyric poet rather than as a prophet) can be traced (quite apart from the fairly unimportant fact that Miss Dickinson, in her apprenticeship, closely imitated Blake's form in at least two poems). Both took over the simplest forms of the song and the hymn and turned this simplicity to their own uses. Both seemed to work straight from almost dictated inspiration (Blake, indeed, claimed that his poems were dictated to him intact and entire) but we now know, from an examination of their manuscripts, that both worked over their original drafts with meticulous care. Both had to struggle against hampering circumstances: Blake against poverty and misunderstanding, and Dickinson against a lack of true response in the traditionally stiffened society in which she found herself. To both poets, limitation and boundary finally yielded originality and power; they were sufficiently outside the spirit of their times so that they were comparatively untouched by the vagaries of fashion; they both were able to wring from solitary contemplation sound working principles and just form. . . .

This power to say the unsayable—to hint of the unknowable—is the power of the seer, in this woman equipped with an ironic intelligence and great courage of spirit. The stuff of Emily Dickinson's imagination is of this world; there is nothing macabre about her material (in the manner of Poe) and there is very little of the labored or artificial about her means. If "she mastered life by rejecting it," she mastered that Nature concerning which she had such ambivalent feeling by adding herself to the sum of all things, in a Rilkean habit of praise. "She kept in touch with reality," someone has said of her, "by the clearest and finest of the senses—the sense of sight. Perhaps the great vitality of contact by vision is the essence, in part, of her originality." How exactly she renders the creatures of this earth! She gives them to us, not as symbols of this or that, but as themselves. And her lyrical notation is so precise, so fine and moves so closely in union with her mind, that she is continually striking out aphorisms, from Plotinus to Blake. And as her life goes on, everything becomes whittled down, evanescent. Her handwriting becomes a kind of fluid print; her poems become notations; all seems to be on the point of disappearing. And suddenly all disappears. . . .

"My business is to create," said the poet Blake. "My business is circumference," said the poet Dickinson. And we know that the physical center of that circumference was to remain the town of Amherst, which almost exactly one hundred years ago (on December 10th, 1859) Miss Dickinson described with great charm and deep affection, in a letter to Mrs. Samuel Bowles: "It storms in Amherst five days—it snows, and then it rains, and then soft fogs like vails hang on all the houses, and then the days turn Topaz, like a lady's pin . . ."— as delicate a description as a New England town and New England winter weather have ever received.

From *Emily Dickinson: Three Views* (Amherst: Amherst College Press, 1960), pp. 27-34.

SISTER MARY HUMILIATA

A Mystic Poet?

WHAT IS striking in the work of Emily Dickinson as one searches it for her beliefs is the frank, thoughtful, sometimes playful, but always direct approach which she makes to the problems of life, death, and immortality. Her concern with these problems and her expression of the judgments she has made in her own highly individualistic idiom has probably led to the classification of much of her poetry as mystical.

A brief summary of the principles of mysticism as found in the mystical writers of all times will assist in ascertaining what qualities are, in general, characteristic of their work. The application of these principles to the work of Miss Dickinson will not lead to incontestable conclusions, but the process may be valuable in indicating the position of this great lyricist in our literature. . . .

Such summaries must, of necessity, represent only the bare outlines of the ideas of mysticism which have been represented in writings throughout the history of its literature. It is useful, also to note the essential nature of the Christian mystic as distinct from the non-Christian mystic. The three main stages of all mysticism, purgation, contemplation, and union, are developed into the three "ways" of the Christian mystic: purgative, illuminative, and unitive. Essentially, however, Christian mysticism differs from non-Christian mysticism chiefly through the Christian belief in the Incarnation of Christ. The Christian mystic possesses a model, an inspiration, a mediator, and an object of his personal love in the Person of Jesus Christ. Further, the purificatory process in Christian mysticism is not that of the Platonic ascent, which was "rarely more than a freedom from the senses to ensure that virtue and wisdom necessary for intellectual contemplation and ascent to the simple purity of the Absolute."[1] For the Christian mystic holds the doctrine of sin, and he is intensely concerned with his personal guilt. Sin, as related to the Incarnation and the Redemption, inspires in him a sense not only of shame but of sorrow and of love as well.

With these ideas in mind, one returns to the poetry of Emily Dickinson. It is the relation of her soul to what she conceived as Absolute Reality which must occupy us first. If we may except a few flippant references, the poetry seems to manifest a sincere and abiding faith in God. Her ideas of God appear

---

1. Joseph Collins, *Christian Mysticism in the Elizabethan Age* (Baltimore: Johns Hopkins Press, 1940), p. 19.

to fluctuate. At times the childlike attitude prevails, and one has a curious mixture of the sophistication and innocence of Miss Dickinson. . . .

One need not doubt that Emily Dickinson believed in God and in the things of the spirit. But that such belief was enriched by contemplative vision of Him, or even a desire for such vision, is very much to be doubted. Death and heaven were the objects of constant speculation by Miss Dickinson, almost to the point of obsession, but the speculation was not that communion with the Divine which the mystic longs for; it was imaginative and entirely based upon sensory experience. Such thoughts are found in "Great streets of silence led away," "I went to heaven—," "I died for beauty," "Safe in their alabaster chambers," "Ample make this bed," and "What inn is this," as well as many others. Death is seen in these poems as inevitable, its experience indefinable except in terms of what we know on earth. Union with God was to be reserved until death, for there was no venture into the supernatural beyond the realm of ideas for Emily Dickinson. For this reason, probably, there is none of that longing for death which the mystic expresses, the result of his communings with God while he remains in the flesh. . . .

References to Christ in the poems of Emily Dickinson are usually not directly concerned with the Person of Christ but rather with some symbol:

> Defeat whets victory, they say;
> The reefs in old Gethsemane
> Endear the shore beyond.
>
> (313—*Poems*, 1891, pp. 46-47)

There are, however, a few exceptions. A spirit of Christian resignation which joins the individual's sufferings to those of Christ is found in:

> I shall know why, when time is over,
> And I have ceased to wonder why;
> Christ will explain each separate anguish
> In the fair schoolroom of the sky.
>
> He will tell me what Peter promised,
> And I, for wonder at his woe,
> I shall forget the drop of anguish
> That scalds me now, that scalds me now.
>
> (193—*Poems*, 1890, p. 151)

This is a religious sentiment and a philosophical adjustment of attitude toward suffering. It is not, however, a mystical document; for, while the Christian practices resignation under the burden of grief and trial, the mystic, the saint—enamored of Christ and anxious to resemble Him—begs for the privilege of pain. Thus St. Theresa of Avila could cry out: "To suffer or to die," and three centuries later, St. Thérèse of Lisieux could say: "Like Thee, O Adorable Spouse, I would be scourged, I would be crucified!" And while these

wrote of the martyrs with a burning desire to share their sacrifice, Miss
Dickinson writes with strong appreciation but with detachment:

> Through the straight pass of suffering
> The martyrs even trod,
> Their feet upon temptation,
> Their faces upon God.
>
> A stately, shriven company;
> Convulsion playing round,
> Harmless as streaks of meteor
> Upon a planet's bound.
>
> Their faith the everlasting troth;
> Their expectation fair;
> The needle to the north degree
> Wades so, through polar air.
>
> (792—*Poems*, 1891, p. 33)

So far as one can penetrate the poetic mind and achievement of Emily
Dickinson, one finds that her work on themes which might be designated as
mystical in nature, her poetry concerned with the Creator, the Redeemer, with
death and immortality, are the fruit of a peculiarly deep insight and an intensely
emotional nature, but they are not of the body of that literature which is based
on the search of the mystic for God and for union with Him. There is faith,
certainly, and religious conviction; but nowhere is there that complete dedication to the search for perfection which motivates the mystic.

Mystic literature, as we have seen, is most often concerned with the metho-
dology of mysticism. To describe the unitive way is a task which has proven
impossible for most mystics. But the way of purgation, especially, has been
fruitful of much of the most graphic of our mystical writing. In both Christian
and non-Christian mystical literature there is a deliberate withdrawal from the
external things of life in order that attention may be centered on the one thing
necessary. In the Christian this purification is motivated by his sense of sin,
but it goes much further than the conscientious effort to rid himself of sin
which is the duty of every Christian. For the mystic there is a deliberate choice
of a difficult self-training, and it is this which constitutes the asceticism of the
genuine mystic.

> . . . The world is full of many beautiful and absorbing things that for
> most men are not only innocent, but profitable; yet they are not what
> he is seeking. There are people in the world to call forth his great faculty
> of love . . . .but he is not seeking men. All the things interesting and
> beautiful and lovable he is gifted to appreciate better than most men; but
> what he is seeking is incomparably more interesting and beautiful and
> lovable. . . . So he leaves the things that warm the lives of other men and
> goes forth on a lonelier and a stricter way.[2]

2. Helen C. White, *The Mysticism of Blake* (Madison, 1927), p. 69.

In Emily Dickinson's poetry one finds indeed that intense sensitivity to experience which is characteristic of the mystic. Her self-chosen isolation from the world might easily be interpreted as the retirement for contemplation which the mystics practice. But the writing which came out of this solitude does not tell the story of the mystic quest. The motive for the secluded life is blurred a little in the biographies, but for present purposes it is not that life which one wishes to judge for its mystic experience but rather the poetry for its expression thereof. And, as far as one can perceive, the poems seem to evoke the picture of one whose intellectual and emotional equipment for life was extraordinary in perception and depth. There is a deliberate contraction of the circle of experience, but within that circle the ultimate meaning of each act is traced to its end. Experience is related to experience by metaphor; intense conviction of truth is pointed by personification, but there is never the deliberate putting-by even of the infinitesimal which is the asceticism of the mystic. Miss Dickinson's assertion: "The time to live is frugal, and good as it is a better earth will not quite be this" is not the statement of an ascetic.

Intellectual discipline in Miss Dickinson means precision of thought and adequate relationship of the unique happening to its place in her scheme of things; it is not the withdrawal into contemplation by which the mystic seeks to establish contact with Ultimate Reality. Her immediate goal, poetic expression, is defined in her own lines:

> This was a Poet—it is that
> Distils amazing sense
> From ordinary meanings,
> And attars so immense
> From the familiar species
> That perished by the door,
> We wonder it was not ourselves
> Arrested it before.
>
> (448—*Further Poems*, 1929, p. 12)

One searches in vain for the more particular signs of the Christian mystic in the poetry of Emily Dickinson. The expression of personal guilt for sin, the feeling of Christian humility, the symbol of earthly love used to explain the Divine, the ecstatic joy of union, and the utter desolation of the "dark nights of the soul"—all these are recorded in the writings of the great mystics, but they are not found in the poetry of Emily Dickinson. Mystical poetry—in the traditional sense, at least—is not Miss Dickinson's poetic gift. To make such a statement is not, however, to deny either her goodness or her genius.

From "Emily Dickinson Mystic Poet?" *College English,* 12 (1950), 144-49.

SUZANNE M. WILSON

Structural Patterns in the Poetry of Emily Dickinson

WHETHER OR not Emily Dickinson's poetry contains definite structural patterns is a matter of considerable scholarly importance and bears strongly on any attempt to evaluate her work aesthetically; establishing technical range is generally a starting point in determining the quality and nature of any artist's performance as an artist. As well, any attempt to judge whether this or that poem in the Dickinson canon is the product of refinement of technique or of a happy or unhappy accident simply cannot be made without first determining whether or not she habitually cast her thought into certain demonstrable patterns which were capable of refinement. As a consequence, upon the question of pattern rests the question of whether or not Emily Dickinson was, as some critics believe, an "instinctive," "automatic" writer whose knowledge of her craft and of her own method of working was negligible or entirely inadequate.

A structural analysis of all the poems in the canon casts a good bit of light on the difficult aesthetic questions posed by her work by revealing a clearly definable range and distribution of patterns. A tabulation of the structural characteristics in the entire canon indicates that one major pattern predominates, that several well-defined variations of this pattern are present, and that the chronological distribution of this pattern in its several variations shows experiment and development in technique and consequently very strongly suggests conscious artistry.

I

The major structural plan or ordering of logical elements conforms to that most commonly found in the sermon and consists of three parts: statement or introduction of topic, elaboration, and conclusion. The high rate of incidence of this pattern contributes, of course, to that "quasi-homiletic" quality apparent to most students of Emily Dickinson's work. The constantly repeated variations of this major pattern are three in number. In the first variation the poet makes her initial announcement of topic in an unfigured line; in the second she uses a figure for that purpose. The third variation is one in which she repeats her statement and its elaboration a number of times before drawing a conclusion.

The simplest combination is that in which the introductory statement is made in a line containing no figures. One of the clearest examples of the type is poem 329:

So glad we are—a Stranger'd deem
'Twas sorry that we were—
For where the Holiday should be
There publishes a Tear—
Nor how Ourselves be justified—
Since Grief and Joy are done
So similar—An Optizan
Could not decide between—[1]

The structural divisions of the poem are simple and clear. In the first two lines
she announces her point; then she illustrates it in an image in the next two
lines. With the peculiar locution in the fifth line she begins her commentary
and uses an image to illustrate it.

II

The second variation, the one the poet most often uses, is that in which she
presents her initial statement of topic in a figure. Consider, for example, poem
319:

The nearest Dream recedes—unrealized—
The Heaven we chase,
Like the June Bee—before the School Boy,
Invites the Race—
Stoops—to an easy Clover—
Dips—evades—teases—deploys—
Then—to the Royal Clouds
Lifts his light Pinnace—
Heedless of the Boy—
Staring—bewildered—at the mocking sky—

Homesick for steadfast Honey—
Ah, the Bee flies not
That brews that rare variety!

Instead of stating her point, illustrating it simply, and making a comment about
it, the poet presents her idea in a figure, moves into a lengthy comparison and
then makes a brief comment.

The number of stanzas and proliferation of imagery, apparently, are not
considerations when we are dealing with Emily Dickinson's structural patterns.
Poem 401, for example, although considerably longer and more complicated
than 319 has substantially the same pattern. In the first stanza she states her

---

1. The numbering and dating of poems in the three-volume Johnson edition (Cambridge, Mass.,
1955) is followed throughout this study, and the poems are transcribed here exactly as they appear
in that edition.

point in two lines charged with overtones and then immediately moves into images which emphasize and enlarge the suggestions presented in lines one and two:

> What Soft—Cherubic Creatures—
> These Gentlewomen are—
> One would as soon assault a Plush—
> Or violate a Star—

The second stanza elaborates further the limitations of the ladies in question:

> Such Dimity Convictions—
> A Horror so refined
> Of freckled Human Nature—
> Of Deity—ashamed—

The third stanza is a commentary on the ideas introduced and elaborated in the first two stanzas:

> It's such a common—Glory—
> A Fisherman's—Degree—
> Redemption—Brittle Lady—
> Be so—ashamed of Thee—

A very interesting use of imagery as a structural component appears in some of Miss Dickinson's poems and is most readily seen functionally in poem 318, where it appears in combination with a section fashioned according to the blueprint of the second variation:

> I'll tell you how the Sun rose—
> A Ribbon at a time—
> The Steeples swam in Amethyst—
> The news, like Squirrels, ran—
> The Hills untied their Bonnets—
> The Bobolinks—begun—
> Then I said softly to myself—
> "That must have been the Sun!"
> But how he set—I know not—
> There seemed a purple stile
> That little Yellow boys and girls
> Were climbing all the while—
> Till when they reached the other side,
> A Dominie in Gray—
> Put gently up the evening Bars—
> And led the flock away—

The first eight lines form a similar pattern of instruction, elaboration, and conclusion. Lines one and two state the point in a figure, and the imagery employed in lines three through six is entirely illustrative. Lines seven and eight form a commentary, and the poem could have ended there. From a structural point of view, the last half of the poem is particularly interesting, however, for here she begins the entire pattern over again, makes her statement, draws a peaceful picture tied nicely to the "Ribbon" imagery in the first part of the poem, but reaches no explicit final conclusion. Her description of nightfall contains an indirect suggested conclusion, however. The last seven lines, or elaboration section of the second half of the poem, tell a little story which resembles a painting and which uses persons to stand for the play of light at evening time. The "purple stile" emphasizes the horizontal as well as the vertical effect of nightfall and also echoes "Amethyst" in line three. The phrase "little Yellow boys and girls" is reminiscent of the image in line two but supplies the color, broken-line effect, and direction of movement of the ribbons of light withdrawing or crawling up over the stile of landscape and houses. Staying with her use of persons, the poet calls twilight "A Dominie in Gray" who, completing the horizontal ribbon imagery begun in 'stile," puts up "the evening Bars" and takes the light completely away. She could have made a number of comments on this picture but she did not have to. Her imagery made it for her, implicitly. The picture of children climbing a stile and being met by a Dominie who is gentle when he drops night and leads his flock back home into light suggests, among other things, the Good Shepherd story and is, in its slow and quiet movement, a kind of benediction *urbis et orbis*.

III

Poem 324 is an excellent example of the third variation in which the poet repeats her statement and its elaboration a number of times before drawing her conclusion. The first stanza announces the theme and shores it up with illustrative imagery:

> Some keep the Sabbath going to Church—
> I keep it staying at Home—
> With a Bobolink for a Chorister—
> And an Orchard, for a Dome—

In the second stanza she repeats this pattern and picks up for the terms of her comparisons the kind of church service and architectural particulars used in the first illustration, thereby binding stanza two to stanza one and underlining again the first two lines of stanza one:

> Some keep the Sabbath in Surplice—
> I just wear my Wings—
> And instead of tolling the Bell, for Church,
> Our little Sexton—sings.

The third stanza continues the enumeration and comparison of particulars of religious observance and contains a commentary on the relative merits of institutional and personal ritual:

> God preaches, a noted Clergyman—
> And the sermon is never long,
> So instead of going to Heaven, at last—
> I'm going, all along.

IV

The chronological distribution of this pattern and its major variations indicates a line of development proceeding from structural apprenticeship and experiment to consolidation and sophistication of performance. In the poetry written before 1862 we find two groups of poems—those assembled into packets and those antedating the packet assembly of 1858. The structural patterns displayed in these very early poems are clear, if sometimes elaborate, examples of the first two variations of the statement-elaboration-conclusion pattern, and all three variations are evident in the packet poetry. The explicitness of the structural components seems to indicate, however, that at this point the poet was not yet able to substitute implicit for explicit structure by means of word association in her imagery.

The poetry of 1862 represents a continuation of basic variations plus the substitution of an implicit conclusion through imagery for an explicit commentary. The poems written in the period 1863-1865 represent a slight narrowing of her exploration of the possibilities of some variations and a consolidating of experiment. And those poems written during the last twenty years of her life represent an even further consolidation; in these poems we find the variations of the statement-elaboration-conclusion limited substantially to two, the repetition variation having been eliminated.

Even if we consider the dating of the poems in the Dickinson canon to be only approximations, and Thomas Johnson quite honestly uses the term "about" when it seems wise to him to do so, we nevertheless see a pattern of structural experiment and development in these poems which seems to indicate that she had some clear notion, structurally at least, of what she was doing and wanted to do. That the basic sermon pattern itself might be "automatic" or "instinctive" depends upon the way in which one interprets those words. Certainly the poet's exposure to the tradition of the Protestant New England sermon cannot be denied. What we know of her life, training, and contacts with other New Englanders could certainly lead us to say that the basic organization she uses could be considered perfectly "natural" for her if not thoroughly normal and to be expected in the time and area in which she lived. The pattern of experiment with this basic organization indicates design and manipulation, however, and these indicate conscious artistry. . . .

From "Structural Patterns in the Poetry of Emily Dickinson," *American Literature,* 35 (May, 1963), 53-59.

Explications

NANCY LENZ HARVEY

"What Soft Cherubic Creatures"

What Soft—Cherubic Creatures—
These Gentlewomen are—
One would as soon assault a Plush—
Or violate a Star—

Such Dimity Convictions—
A Horror so refined
Of freckled Human Nature—
Of Deity—ashamed—

It's such a common—Glory—
A Fisherman's—Degree—
Redemption—Brittle Lady—
Be so—ashamed of Thee—

EMILY DICKINSON'S "What Soft Cherubic Creatures" (# 401 in the Johnson edition) is a stinging denunciation of the hypocrisy embodied in gentlewomen. Although they appear delicate and remote—"One would as soon assault a Plush / Or violate a Star" (lines 3-4)—these ladies are neither soft nor cherubic. Their very label is a misnomer; their invective against humankind and the Godhead is anything but gentle. This first stanza is then both caustic and satirical.

The second stanza explicates reasons for the poet's tone. These ladies with their dainty, delicate, "dimity" convictions and their "refined" horror are abashed by "freckled Human Nature" (lines 5-7). Human nature, besmirched by original sin, contains within it all the *ugliness* of the flesh, sin and sex—ideas abhorrent to the *gentler* sort. Yet as the ladies shame the flesh, they inadvertently shame the Deity, for man is made in God's image.

These first two stanzas seem to be clear and straightforward, while the third and final stanza becomes curiously ambiguous, and the punctuation of stanzas 2 and 3 increases this ambiguity. If the lines "It's such a common—glory—/ A Fisherman's—Degree—" (lines 9-10) are read as part of those "Dimity Convictions," the flesh is condemned once more because it is a *common* glory —a second-rate glory. It is thus of low estate, that level of society known only to the laborer, the "fisherman's degree." The words *common* and *degree* are often spouted by those who feel themselves remote from the herd, who fail to see a humanity basic to all men.

If, however, these lines begin another thought, then the poem moves progressively to a theological note, and the diction—"common glory," "fisherman's degree," and "redemption"—reinforces this note. Not only are the ladies in horror of human nature, made in the image of God, but they have also failed to realize that human nature is the common or shared glory of God and man. This is the nature chosen by God as He becomes the man Jesus— the man who is a fisher of men. Since the purpose of Christ's life and passion is solely for the redemption of human nature, the closing lines are closely related to the poem as a whole. The ladies are now rightly called: they are "brittle" ladies capable of meanness and sharp cruelty; for they have not only denied the humanity of others and of themselves, but they have also denied their God. Redemption, if now, would "be ashamed" of them.

The rich ambiguity of this last stanza tightens the unity of the poem. The theological reading strengthens the tie of the last two lines to the poem as a whole and combines with the other reading to underscore the superciliousness of the ladies. The cherubic ladies of the opening line become nothing less than alienated creatures who have so distanced themselves from both God and man that they are more *mineral* than *human*—they are brittle creatures.

From "Dickinson's 'What Soft Cherubic Creatures,' " *The Explicator,* 28 (1969-70), Item 27.

CLEANTH BROOKS
AND ROBERT PENN WARREN

"After great pain, a formal feeling comes"

After great pain, a formal feeling comes—
The Nerves sit ceremonious, like Tombs—
The stiff Heart questions was it He, that bore,
And Yesterday, or Centuries before?

The Feet, mechanical, go round—
Of Ground, or Air, or Ought—
A Wooden way
Regardless grown,
A Quartz contentment, like a stone—

This is the Hour of Lead—
Remembered, if outlived,
As Freezing persons, recollect the Snow—
First—Chill—then Stupor—then the letting go—

. . . The pain is obviously not a physical pain; it is some great sorrow or mental pain which leaves the mind numbed. The nerves, she says, "sit ceremonious like tombs." The word *sit* is very important here. The nerves, it is implied, are like a group of people after a funeral sitting in the parlor in a formal hush. Then the poet changes the image slightly by adding "like tombs." The nerves are thus compared to two different things, but each of the comparisons contributes to the same effect, and indeed are closely related: people dressed in black sitting around a room after a funeral may be said to be like tombs. And why does the reference to "tombs" seem such a good symbol for a person who has just suffered great pain (whether it be a real person or the nerves of such a person personified)? Because a tomb has to a supreme degree the qualities of deadness (quietness, stillness) and of formality (ceremony, stiffness).

Notice that the imagery (through the first line of the last stanza) is characterized by the possession of a common quality, the quality of *stiff lifelessness.* For instance, the heart is "stiff," the feet walk a "wooden" way, the contentment is a "quartz" contentment, the hour is that of "lead." The insistence on this type of imagery is very important in confirming the sense of numbed consciousness which is made more explicit by the statement that the feet move mechanically and are "regardless" of where they go. Notice too that the lines are bound together, not only by the constant reference of the imagery to the result of grief, but also by the fact that the poet is stating in series what happens to the parts of the body: nerves, heart, feet.

Two special passages in the first two stanzas deserve additional comment before we pass on to the third stanza. The capital letter in the word *He* tells us that Christ is meant. The heart, obsessed with pain and having lost the sense of time and place, asks whether it was Christ who bore the cross. The question is abrupt and elliptic as though uttered at a moment of pain. And the heart asks whether it is not experiencing His pain, and—having lost hold of the real world—whether the crucifixion took place yesterday or centuries before. And behind these questions lies the implication that pain is a constant part of the human lot. The implied figure of a funeral makes the heart's question about the crucifixion come as an appropriate one, and the quality of the suffering makes the connection implied between its own sufferings and that on the cross not violently farfetched.

The line, "A quartz contentment like a stone," is particularly interesting. The comparison involves two things. First, we see an extension of the common association of stoniness with the numbness of grief, as in such phrases as "stony-eyed" or "heart like a stone," etc. But why does the poet use "quartz"? There are several reasons. The name of the stone helps to particularize the figure and prevent the effect of cliche. Moreover, quartz is a very hard stone. And, for one who knows that quartz is a crystal, a "quartz contentment" is a contentment crystalized, as it were, out of the pain. This brings us to the second general aspect involved by the comparison. This aspect is ironical. The contentment arising after the shock of great pain is a contentment because of the inability to respond any longer, rather that the ability to respond satisfactorily and agreeably.

To summarize for a moment, the poet has developed an effect of inanimate lifelessness, a stony, or wooden, or leaden stiffness; now, she proceeds to use a new figure, that of the freezing person, which epitomizes the effect of those which have proceeded it, but which also gives a fresh and powerful statement.

The line, "Remembered if outlived," is particularly forceful. The implication is that few outlive the experience to be able to remember and recount it to others. This experience of grief is like a death by freezing: there is the chill, then the stupor as the body becomes numbed, and then the last state in which the body finally gives up the fight against the cold, and relaxes and dies. The correspondence of the stages of death by freezing to the effect of the shock of deep grief on the mind is close enough to make the passage very powerful. But there is another reason for the effect which this last figure has on us. The imagery of the first two stanzas corresponds to the "stupor." The last line carries a new twist of idea, one which supplies a context for the preceding imagery and which by explaining it, makes it more meaningful. The formality, the stiffness, the numbness of the first two stanzas is accounted for: it is an attempt to hold in, the fight of the mind against letting go; it is a defense of the mind.

From *Understanding Poetry* (1938); rpt. in *Fourteen by Emily Dickinson: With Selected Criticism*, ed. Thomas M. Davis, Fair Lawn, N. J.: Scott Foresman, 1964), pp. 49-51.

CHARLES ANDERSON

"There's a certain Slant of light"

THE ULTIMATE problem, then, was not to master despair, which she presumably succeeded in doing as a woman when she took the artist's path to peace, but to manage the images evoked by her sensibility so as to transform the experience into great poetry. The . . . technique . . . was brought under perfect control in her finest poem on despair:

> There's a certain Slant of light,
> Winter Afternoons—
> That oppresses, like the Heft
> Of Cathedral Tunes—
>
> Heavenly Hurt, it gives us—
> We can find no scar,
> But internal difference,
> Where the Meanings, are—
>
> None may teach it—Any—
> 'Tis the Seal Despair—
> An imperial affliction
> Sent us of the Air—
>
> When it comes, the Landscape listens—
> Shadows—hold their breath—
> When it goes, 'tis like the Distance
> On the look of Death—

For more than half a century this poem was placed by her editors under the category of nature. But winter sunlight is simply the over-image of despair, inclosing the center of suffering that is her concern. Grammatically, the antecedent of the neutral 'it' whose transformations make up the action of the poem is this 'certain Slant' of light, but in figurative meaning 'it' is the 'Heavenly Hurt.' This is a true metaphor, sensation and abstraction fused into one, separable in logic but indistinguishable and even reversible in a poetic sense. The internal experience is not talked about but is realized in a web of images that constitutes the poem's statement, beginning with one drawn from nature, or rather from the firmament above it, and returning to it in the end with significant change of meaning.

These multiple images exemplifying the protean condition of despair are vividly discrete, but they grow out of each other and into each other with a fitness that creates the intended meaning in shock after shock of recognition. Its amorphous quality is embodied at the outset in 'light,' a diffused substance that can be apprehended but not grasped. Further, this is a slanting light, as uncertain of source and indirect in impact as the feeling of despair often is. Finally, it is that pale light of 'Winter Afternoons,' when both the day and the year seem to be going down to death, the seasonal opposite of summer which symbolized for her the fullness and joy of living. It is when he feels winter in his soul, one remembers, that Melville's Ishmael begins his exploration of the meaning of despair. Next, by the shift of simile, this desolation becomes 'like the Heft/Of Cathedral Tunes.' The nebulous has now been made palpable, by converting light waves into sound waves whose weight can be felt by the whole body. The strong provincialism, 'Heft' (smoothed away to 'Weight' by former editors), carries both the meaning of ponderousness and the great effort of heaving in order to test it, according to her Lexicon. This homely word also clashes effectively with the grand ring of 'Cathedral Tunes,' those produced by carillon offering the richest possibilities of meaning. Since this music 'oppresses,' the connotation of funereal is added to the heavy resonance of all pealing bells. And since the double meaning of 'Heft' carries through, despair is likened to both the weight of these sounds on the spirit and the straining to lift the imponderable tonnage of cast bronze.

The religious note on which the prelude ends, 'Cathedral Tunes,' is echoed in the language of the central stanzas. In its ambiguousness 'Heavenly Hurt' could refer to the pain of paradisiac ecstasy, but more immediately this seems to be an adjective of agency, from heaven, rather than an attributive one. The hurt is inflicted from above, 'Sent us of the Air,' like the 'Slant of light' that is its antecedent. In this context that natural image takes on a new meaning, again with the aid of her Lexicon which gives only one meaning for 'slant' as a noun, 'an oblique reflection or gibe.' It is then a mocking light, like the heavenly hurt that comes from the sudden instinctive awareness of man's lot since the Fall, doomed to mortality and irremediable suffering. This is indeed despair, though not in the theological sense unless Redemption is denied also. As Gerard Manley Hopkins phrases it in 'Spring and Fall,' for the young life there coming to a similar realization, 'It is the blight man was born for.'

Because of this it is beyond human correction, 'None may teach it—Any.' Though it penetrates it leaves 'no scar,' as an outward sign of healing, nor any internal wound that can be located and alleviated. What it leaves is 'internal difference,' the mark of all significant 'Meanings.' When the psyche is once striken with the pain of such knowledge it can never be the same again. The change is final and irrevocable, sealed. The Biblical sign by which God claims man for his own has been shown in the poems of heavenly bridal to be a 'Seal,' the ring by which the beloved is married into immortal life. But to be redeemed one must first be mortal, and be made conscious of one's mortality. The initial and overwhelming impact of this can lead to a state of hopelessness, unaware that the 'Seal Despair' might be the reverse side of the seal of ecstasy. So, when first stamped on the consciousness it is an 'affliction.' But it is also 'imperial . . . Sent us of the Air,' the heavenly kingdom where God sits enthroned, and from the same source can come Redemption, though not in this poem.

By an easy transition from one insubstantial image to another, 'Air' back to 'a certain Slant of light,' the concluding stanza returns to the surface level of the winter afternoon. As the sun drops toward the horizon just before setting, 'the Landscape listens' in apprehension that the very light which makes it exist as a landscape is about to be extinguished; 'Shadows,' which are about to run out to infinity in length and merge with each other in breadth until all is shadow, 'hold their breath.' This is the effect created by the slanting light 'When it comes.' Of course no such things happen in nature, and it would be pathetic fallacy to pretend they did. The light does not inflict this suffering nor is the landscape the victim. Instead, these are just images of despair.

Similar figures are used in two other poems. In one the declining motion of the sun seems just a symbol of the inexorability of death:

> Presentiment—is that long Shadow—on the Lawn—
> Indicative that Suns go down—
>
> The Notice to the startled Grass
> That Darkness—is about to pass—

But in relation to the whole body of her poetry such apprehensiveness of the coming of 'Darkness,' like a dreaded king whose approach has already been heralded, suggests that this 'Presentiment' is one of unbearable pain. In the other poem it is so named. When lives are assailed by little anguish they merely 'fret,' she says, but when threatened with 'Avalanches . . . they'll slant,'

> Straighten—look cautious for their Breath—
> But make no syllable—like Death—

So with the slant of light 'When it goes,' as the sun finally sets and darkness covers all, "tis like the Distance/On the look of Death.' Such is the difference between the coming of despair and the aftermath of extinction. The latter calls up an image of the staring eyes of the dead, the awful 'Distance' between life and death, and, as the only relief in sight, the distance between the poet and her experience that has made this sure control of form and language possible. The final and complete desolation of the landscape is the precise equivalent of that 'internal difference' which the action of the poem has brought about.

From *Emily Dickinson's Poetry: Stairway of Surprise* (New York: Holt, Rinehart and Winston, 1960), pp. 215-18.

THOMAS H. JOHNSON

"Because I could not stop for Death"

IN 1863 Death came into full stature as a person. "Because I could not stop for Death" is a superlative achievement wherein Death becomes one of the great characters of literature.

It is almost impossible in any critique to define exactly the kind of reality which her character Death attains, simply because the protean shifts of form are intended to forestall definition. A poem can convey the nuances of exultation, agony, compassion, or any mystical mood. But no one can successfully define mysticism because the logic of language has no place for it. One must therefore assume that the reality of Death, as Emily Dickinson conceived him, is to be perceived by the reader in the poems themselves. Any analysis can do no more than suggest what may be looked for.

In "Because I could not stop for Death" Emily Dickinson envisions Death as a person she knew and trusted, or believed that she could trust. He might be any Amherst gentleman . . . who at one time or another had acted as her squire.

> Because I could not stop for Death—
> He kindly stopped for me—
> The Carriage held but just Ourselves—
> And Immortality.

The carriage holds but the two of them, yet the ride, as she states with quiet emphasis, is a last ride together. Clearly there has been no deception on his part. They drive in a leisurely manner, and she feels completely at ease. Since she understands it to be a last ride, she of course expects it to be unhurried. Indeed, his graciousness in taking time to stop for her at that point and on that day in her life when she was so busy she could not possibly have taken time to stop for him, is a mark of special politeness. She is therefore quite willing to put aside her work. And again, since it is to be her last ride, she can dispense with her spare moments as well as her active ones.

> We slowly drove—He knew no haste
> And I had put away
> My labor and my leisure too
> For His Civility—

She notes the daily routine of the life she is passing from. Children playing games during a school recess catch her eye at the last. And now the sense of motion is quickened. Or perhaps more exactly one should say that the sense of time comes to an end as they pass the cycles of the day and the seasons of the year, at a period of both ripeness and decline.

> We passed the School, where Children strove
> At Recess—in the Ring—
> We passed the Fields of Gazing Grain—
> We passed the Setting Sun—

How insistently "passed" echoes through the stanza! She now conveys her feeling of being outside time and change, for she corrects herself to say that the sun passed them, as it of course does all who are in the grave. She is aware of dampness and cold, and becomes suddenly conscious of the sheerness of the dress and scarf which she now discovers that she wears.

> Or rather—He passed Us—
> The Dews drew quivering and chill—
> For only Gossamer, my Gown—
> My Tippet—only Tulle—

The two concluding stanzas, with progressively decreasing concreteness, hasten the final identification of her "House." It is the slightly rounded surface "of the Ground," with a scarcely visible roof and a cornice "in the Ground." To time and seasonal change, which have already ceased, is now added motion. Cessation of all activity and creativeness is absolute. At the end, in a final instantaneous flash of memory, she recalls the last objects before her eyes during the journey: the heads of the horses that bore her, as she had surmised they were doing from the beginning, toward—it is the last word—"Eternity."

> We paused before a House that seemed
> A Swelling of the Ground—
> The Roof was scarcely visible—
> The Cornice—in the Ground—
>
> Since then—'tis Centuries—and yet
> Feels shorter than the Day
> I first surmised the Horses Heads
> Were toward Eternity—

Gradually, too, one realizes that Death as a person has receded into the background, mentioned last only impersonally in the opening words "We paused" of the fifth stanza, where his services as squire and companion are over. In this poem concrete realism melds into "awe and circumference" with matchless economy.

From *Emily Dickinson: An Interpretive Biography* (Cambridge: Harvard Univ. Press, 1955), pp. 222-24.

ERNEST SANDEEN

Dickinson's Late-Summer Poems

THE DEEP-SEATED concerns which motivate these poems of Indian summer relate them to other poems and groups of poems of Dickinson's which otherwise have no connection with the seasons of the year. For example, the recurring interest she shows in the "last of summer" before it fades into autumn and "dies" into winter is felt to be almost identical with the interest she shows in the last moments of consciousness before her own imagined death in "I heard a Fly buzz—when I died" (No. 465—1862). To corroborate the impression, in both this poem and "Further in Summer" an insect sound is selected to represent the diminution of life in the pause before final extinction.

Of greater interest than their thematic ramifications, however, is the bearing which the late-summer poems have upon Dickinson's creative procedure in general. As we have seen, the "last of summer" is for her the brief moment in which the season stops to contemplate itself, to review, pensively, its past delights and ecstasies, before gliding imperceptibly away into the nonbeing of winter. However, this same two-fold, reflexive movement clearly governs the structure of many of Dickinson's poems in which no reference is made to this season or to any season of the year. In other words, Dickinson's reaction to the late summer, that of "delight deterred by retrospect," describes a psychological model which she follows in creating many if not most of her poems: first, the instantaneous, emotionally urgent response to an experience and second, the interval in which the response is arrested and subjected to searching scrutiny. It is a creative act which comprehends in one process both the initial intuition and the subsequent rational analysis of that intuition.

Including as it does both the subconscious and the conscious processes involved in poetic creation, this procedure can be said merely to describe the way in which all poems are composed. But with Dickinson the dual movement seems to be more deliberate than with most poets and therefore more readily observable or at least more easily inferred. Also, poets differ widely in respect to the point at which in the conversion of the raw materials of their experience into poetic experience they typically produce the actual poem. In general, Dickinson's better poems give evidence that the motivating phenomena have been thoroughly assimilated through the operation of her conscious, critical mind before she begins to write them. What commands her attention is the adjustment of a given occurrence to her own subjective needs and therefore it is the effect which this occurrence has had upon her that she attends to rather than the factual experience itself. A good example is her often anthologized and explicated "After great pain, a formal feeling comes" (No. 341—1862), in which no reference is made to an occasion, or a succession of occasions, which might have given her her knowledge of intense suffering. The particular experience itself is ignored. Her only interest is in analyzing the effect—of such an occasion as the reader is left free to imagine for himself. In fact, she concentrates her analysis on only one temporal segment of the effect the "formal feeling" which follows upon "great pain."[1]

This double movement involving an initial response which is extraordinarily sensitive and an analysis of this response which is subtle and trenchant, as well as scrupulously honest, gives Dickinson's best poems their effect of ambiguous but concentrated power. As Archibald MacLeish has pointed out, they are felt to be intimately personal and at the same time remarkably tough-minded and detached.

Yet whatever "distance" she achieves through her almost clinical examination of her own responses, the examination is itself focussed upon the world of her inner life. Her creative energy is directed inward, is centripetal in its effect just as that of her contemporary, Walt Whitman, is clearly outgoing and centrifugal. Despite his assertions about "absorbing" the people, animals, and things he observes into the depths of his ego, there to be merged in a single "identity" with himself, the only evidence that such a process actually takes place remains solely such assertions. Much more convincing as far as his authority as a poet is concerned, are the catalogues to which he continually reverts, recording his acutely perceived observations of the actual world in which he lives. These make us believe that the mosaic he creates, although he envelops it in his own subjective aura, is really a portrait of the United States of his time, not merely in the humdrum details of its everyday life but in its inarticulate, expansive aspirations. Dickinson's intuitive and analytical power may be as great as his, and like him she is also a realist, but the reality she persuades us to accept is that of her own unique inner self. While Whitman sits and looks out, Emily Dickinson sits and looks in. The illumination that flashes from her best lines does not come from an explosion but from an implosion.

To illustrate the relevance of Dickinson's late-summer poems to the psychological design which shaped much of her poetry, it is well to begin with the best poem of this same series, "Further in Summer than the Birds" (No. 1068—1866), which has been discussed above in another context. Here it will be shown that the season of late August which is the subject of the poem is a metaphor with not only a substantive reference to Dickinson's sense of the relation between life and death but also a purely structural reference to the two-fold movement which forms the poem.

The somber, meditative mood of "Further in Summer" is conventionally autumnal, but the one concrete detail selected to link the mood to the season, namely, the song of the crickets, is so tenuous and is developed through a

---

1. See also No. 701 (1863) "A Thought went up my mind today" and No. 747 (1863) "It dropped so low—in my Regard."

succession of associations so private, that the reader's attention throughout is centered, not on the song, but on the poet's reaction to it.

In the first stanza the sound of the crickets is introduced, without being named, in the religious metaphor on which the whole poem is constructed: "a minor Nation" is celebrating its Mass. Thus from the outset, the cricket song is presented under a figure which does nothing to describe the sound itself but, rather, analyzes the personal associations which the sound has aroused in the poet's mind before the poem begins. The rite is a "pathetic" one, and there is an implied contrast between this "canticle" in the lowly grass and the singing of birds in the treetops at an earlier period—a contrast which suggests how the life of the summer has been diminished and how the tone of the season has changed as a result.

The elaboration of the dominant figure through the rest of the poem shows the poet probing her highly individual sense of the cricket sound. The intensely subjective character of the experience becomes most apparent in the third stanza where the poet asserts that the "spectral Canticle" is "felt" to be "antiquest" at noon. Why the sound of the crickets should be felt as "antique" at all is not explained. Perhaps she is associating with the Mass of the minor nation the idea of the Last Supper, which, as we saw, appears in "These are the days when Birds come back" (No. 130—1859). But more likely the sudden intrusion of the notion of antiquity reflects her perception that this insect sacrament antedates the Christian formulation and is as primitive as nature itself. This suggestion of the prehistoric seems to be reinforced by the esoteric reference in the last stanza to the "Druidic Difference" which the cricket song has created in her awareness of the summer season. Finally, this difference is one which for the poet "enhances Nature." Again, no reason for this effect is given, but knowing her doctrine of gain through loss, we may conjecture that by providing the summer with its sacramental swan song the insect ritual emphasizes for the poet the significance of the season which is already beginning to pass away from her.

The poetic tact which prompted Dickinson to delete the three stanzas which she had initially written to stand between stanzas two and three of the final draft demonstrates her sharpened awareness of her objective. These stanzas are not only generally diffusive in effect; they are diffusive in a particularly distractive way. That is, they turn outward toward the cricket song itself, describing its changes through the course of a night and a day, and so run counter to the movement of the poem which is directed inward, converging upon the poet's introspective interpretation.

The same procedural pattern, the presentation of a highly internalized experience which is at the same time submitted to a detailed analytical examination, is also apparent in Dickinson's best poem on the winter season. Here the single sensuous detail which is isolated from the poet's total experience of "winter afternoons" is given in the first line: "A certain Slant of light" (No. 258—1861). The rest of the poem is a minute investigation, not of the physical slant of light and what it does to the winter scene, but of its unique effect on the poet's sensibility. None of the similes and metaphors in the poem has any intrinsic connection with winter or with light. They are figures of the inner life, analyzing and defining an introspective, not a physical reality. Just as the "spectral Canticle" from the grass induced a "Druidic Difference" in her feeling for the summer though there was no evidence of any outward change in the season, so this wintry slant of light creates "internal difference/Where the Meanings are."

In her famous poem, "A Route of Evanescence" (No. 1463—1879), Dickinson is not moved to such a reflective mood as she was by the cricket song in late August or by a peculiar angle of light on a winter afternoon. Being a creature of summertime movement and life, the hummingbird evoked for her a purely sensuous impression. The difference between this poem and the two poems just discussed is that here the response and its analysis are not, as in the others, expanded into the wider, more abstract area of the poet's feeling about life but are confined to the concrete data of the experience. Yet even within this limited scope of perception, essentially the same psychological structure in the formation of the poem can be discerned: an immediate, penetrating reaction to the given phenomenon combined with an intensive analysis defining that reaction. Thus the whole experience is internalized. Despite the vivid impression of reality it conveys, this hummingbird of the poem is distinctively Dickinson's hummingbird.

Critics have found it useful to bring into their discussion of "A Route" an earlier Dickinson poem, "Within my Garden, rides a Bird" (No. 500—1862) in which having already evolved the images of the revolving wheel and the flowers nodding in the bird's wake, she seems to be striving for the effect she achieved in the later poem. Compared to this earlier "rehearsal," "A Route" represents a reduction of twenty lines to eight lines and so illustrates Dickinson's celebrated economy of diction and imagery when she is writing at the top of her bent. But this condensation also illustrates her perfection of the psychological procedure we have been investigating.

It is obvious that in the shorter poem she has moved away from the immediate occasion of the experience which is more amply recorded in the poem of 1862. The details of the garden setting and such circumstances as the presence of her dog have disappeared. Only the purely subjective effect of the encounter with the bird has been retained in order to be intensified. Precisely as in "Further in Summer" and "There's a certain Slant of light" she concentrates on a single aspect of her experience to convey her perception of the whole experience, and characteristically she announces it in the first line, "A Route of Evanescence." Other attributes of the bird are included, such as its green and red coloration, the sound of its wings, and the movement of its wings so rapid as to resemble the revolving spokes of a wheel, but these are firmly subordinated to the dominant impression of the bird's amazing speed causing it to appear and disappear, as it were, simultaneously. The suggestion in its flight of something dyed in red is expressed as "A *Rush* of Cochineal," and the synesthetic "Resonance of Emerald" indicates that the bird moves so fast that sound and sight are merged in one fleeting sensation. The two more indirect images of the last four lines clearly reinforce the same sense of extraordinary speed.

The syntax of the poem also testifies to the reflexive procedure of a dominant intuitive perception meticulously discriminated and condensed. There is only one complete sentence in the poem, and this does not make a statement about the hummingbird but about the nodding blossoms it leaves behind it. The rest of the poem consists mainly of nouns modified by noun phrases. Formally these are subjects without verbs but semantically they express a lively sense of the bird's movement, especially his speed of movement. In short, Dickinson has created out of these nouns a series of predicates with an understood but never designated subject. This device again emphasizes the main idea of the poem; it suggests that the bird flies too swiftly to be certainly identified and named. The only evidence of its existence is the path of its flight and this seems to vanish at the same instant it is perceived.

In this study of three of her poems, generally recognized as among her best, we have seen how Emily Dickinson contracts, successively, her whole sense of the late summer into the song of the crickets, of dreary winter afternoons into a certain slant of light, and of a hummingbird into its one attribute of breathtaking speed. This compression of her feeling for an affecting experience into the confines of a severely selected segment of that experience has the effect of putting her total response under a great deal of psychological pressure. This procedure like that of her closely related principle of renunciation was a part of the game which she discovered she would have to play if she were to transform her narrow experience of the real world into a significantly compensatory enlargement of her inner life. With her it was a matter, always, of converting her limited experience into the fullness of poetic experience. But in her best poems this process was accompanied by another, that of achieving an analytical detachment which enabled her, in turn, to make of her subjective world of undefined ecstasy and despair a convincing reality.

From "Delight Deterred by Retrospect: Emily Dickinson's Late-Summer Poems," *New England Quarterly*, 40 (1967), 483-500.

BRITA SEYERSTED

"Further in Summer than the Birds"

IN THE foregoing chapters we have observed and analyzed certain aspects of Emily Dickinson's poetic language, focusing on one area of analysis at a time. The role of the speaker and the kind of address the poems present have been dealt with; diction and imagery have received their share of attention, as have prosodic factors and syntactic-rhetorical features. In order to bring these different investigations together and to try to distinguish a unity of purpose and method in the poet's work I shall in these concluding pages analyze one poem from the several aspects that seem relevant to the poetic effect this particular poem achieves—not pretending that one single poem will afford opportunities to discuss all the features of style dealt with in this book.

A proposed explication of a poem may be regarded as "a hypothesis that is tested by its capacity to account for the greatest quantity of data in the words of the poem".[1] The poem I have selected for analysis, "Further in Summer than the Birds" (No. 1068), is one that has been widely praised and interpreted. It has been explicated in several different ways, not just regarding details of phrasing and imagery, etc., but also as to the more pervasive questions of theme and attitude. I have profited greatly from the profound and acute observations and suggestions of my predecessors in this game.[2] When I produce still another explication, it is in the hope that it will contribute a detail or two to that final hypothesis of the poem's meaning which—if we agree with such a theory of explication—we will in the end regard as superior to other alternative hypotheses.[3]

There are three holographs of this poem, two written early in 1866, and one seventeen years later.[4] (There are also extant two transcripts, both longer than the holographs and poetically inferior.[5]) I reprint—with a few marks of punctu-

---

1. Monroe C. Beardsley, *Aesthetics: Problems in the Philosophy of Criticism*, New York, 1958, p. 145.

2. A few explications have been collected in *14 by Emily Dickinson: With Selected Criticism*, ed. Thomas M. Davis, Chicago, 1964, pp. 119-136. The latest to date is by Sidney E. Lind (*American Literature*, XXXIX, May 1967, pp. 163-169) who points out an interesting parallel with Hawthorne's "The Old Manse".

3. Cf. Beardsley (loc. cit.): "... in most poems for which alternative hypotheses can be offered it will turn out in the end that one is superior to the other."

4. For details on the MSS, see *Poems*, II, commentary pp. 753-755; and Anderson, *Emily Dickinson's Poetry*, pp. 324 f.

5. Anderson refers to one as "the 'Vanderbilt' MS" (p. 324): it is, however, not a Dickinson manuscript, but a transcript—as the punctuation clearly indicates—made by Mabel Loomis Todd

ation added—the 1866 copy which Emily Dickinson sent to Colonel Higginson. It is true that in the mid-1860s she used dashes and other marks much less copiously than earlier, but she did not often send off a poem as sparsely punctuated as this one. Since her dashes often suggest how phrases and clauses should be interpreted syntactically and since especially the second stanza of this poem will benefit from such aids, I indicate within parentheses the additional marks of the copy written in 1883. I print alongside the text my analysis of the poem's meter and rhythm:

Further in Summer than the Birds (—)	oó|oó|oò|oó	óo ı oóo ı ooó ʌ
Pathetic from the Grass	oó|oò|oó	oóo ı ooó ʌ
A minor Nation celebrates	oó|oó|oó|oó	oóo ı oó ı óoo ı ...
It's unobtrusive Mass.	oò|oó|oó	oòoóo ı ó ʌ
No Ordinance be seen (—)	oó|oò|oó	óóoo ı oó ʌ
So gradual the Grace	oó|oò|oó	óóoo ı oó ı
A pensive Custom it becomes (—)	oó|oó|oò|oó	oóo ı óo ı òoó ʌ
Enlarging Loneliness.	oó|oó|oó	oóo ı óoo ʌ
Antiquest felt at Noon	oó|oó|oó	oóo ı ó ı oó ʌ
When August burning low	oó|oó|oó	oóo ı óo ı ó ʌ
Arise this spectral Canticle	oó|oó|oó|oó	oó ı oóo ı óoo ʌ
Repose to typify (—)	oó|oó|oó	oó ı oóoo ʌ
Remit as yet no Grace (—)	oó|oó|oò	oó ı oó ı óó ʌ
No Furrow on the Glow (—)	oò|oò|oó	óóo ı oóó ʌ
Yet a Druidic Difference	oó|oó|oó|oó	ó ı oóó ı óoo ı ...
Enhances Nature now (—)	oó|oó|oó	oóo ı óo ı ó ʌ

The subject of the poem is the seasonal change from summer to autumn. The poet describes a premonition of this change as something *heard,* not seen. The sounds of warning that reach an attentive ear are those of the crickets chirping away low down in their miniature universe. We are justified in inferring from external evidence that the "minor Nation" is made up of crickets: in a letter accompanying a copy of this poem Emily Dickinson speaks of it as "My Cricket": she also has other poems on similar themes which name the insects (Nos. 1104, 1271, 1276, 1540 variant, and 1635). The speaker, invisible (note the absence of an "I" in this superior version), stands apart from the crickets' sacred ceremony, having no share in their world. No one in particular is addressed. The poem is not a plea, nor an outburst or a question:

(number Tr 59 in the Bingham Collection at Amherst College). Emily Dickinson presumably sent this poem to Mrs. Gertrude Vanderbilt, either directly or through Susan Dickinson; no such holograph is, however, extant. I am indebted to Mr. J. Richard Phillips, Special Collections Librarian at Amherst College, for information which corroborated my inferences about this transcript.

it is a meditation delivered in a quiet tone. It proceeds from a description of the natural outer world to an intimation of the inner response of the human observer.

For this meditation the poet employs two of her favorite metrical patterns. It opens with a Common Meter stanza which presents actor and action, as well as the time, place, and manner of the action, that is, the crickets' "Mass". The rest of the poem which elaborates on the peculiar character and effect of this mass is framed in the terser Short Meter pattern. The metrical scheme is subtly varied throughout the poem. Initial trochees and frequent variations in degree of stress on the ictus prevent the hymn meter patterns from becoming monotonous. The poem owes its quiet but vital pulsation also—and perhaps more importantly—to the fine tension between meter and rhythm traceable to a fairly great amount of non-coincidence between feet divisions and word and phrase boundaries. Most lines are end-stopped, which lends a certain stability to the verse. The fairly marked pauses at line ends serve to counteract a possible breakdown of order which might have taken place because of a considerable indeterminacy of syntactic structure characterizing some lines—enhanced by the sparseness of punctuation marks.

The rhymes cooperate with the prosodic pattern in establishing a balance between regularity and irregularity. The full rhyme, *Grass-Mass,* appears in the stanza with the greatest number of irregular feet (counting as such other feet than iambs, or iambic feet in which the ictus occurs on a weak syllable, o o). In stanza three there are only two such irregular feet. Counteracting the metrical regularity of this stanza there is the weak sound agreement of a partly unaccented vowel rhyme, *low-typify.* The second and fourth stanzas represent an intermediate state of exactness. The rhyme of stanza two, *Grace-Loneliness,* is fairly "harmonious" (a partly unaccented consonant rhyme with additional similarity between the preceding vowels); in its realization of the metrical scheme this stanza evinces several irregular feet (but fewer than the first stanza). The rhyme of the final stanza, *Glow-now,* is a near-to-perfect sound accord (a vowel rhyme with vowel similarity). The poem is divided into two halves by its rhymes. Stanzas one and two are linked by the final /s/ sounds and the similarity of the preceding vowels. (Note also the alliterative consonant cluster /gr/ and the affinity of the nasals /m/ and /n/ which introduce the rhyming syllables.) The third and fourth stanzas are interrelated by depending on vowels for their sound accord at line ends (*low-Glow-now* forming a close-knit group). The rhymes of this poem do not seem to me to "imitate" the sense of the poem in any notable way. In their blend of exactness and inexactness they contribute to the controlled, but expressive tone that this meditative poem conveys.

Apart from alliteration within lines and across lines and stanzas (*gradual—Grace, Grace—Glow, Repose—Remit,* etc.), specific sounds lend the verse a sonorousness that—like the mass that the poem speaks of—never becomes obtrusive or excessive. The great amount of nasals: /m/, /n/, and (less) /ŋ/; and fricatives: /s/ and /z/, create an illusion of crickets buzzing. The poet speaks elsewhere of how the crickets *sang* (No. 1104); in yet another poem she describes as a *murmuring* the sounds of "some", probably crickets (No. 1115).

The remarkable unity of this poem is not achieved by a logical order of reasoning: nor do parallelism and repetition form a unifying pattern. The unity is created by diction and imagery. The metaphor of the mass dominates the poem, and the words that make up the complex of this metaphor are closely connected through a subtle chain of associations. These progress from the adverb "pathetic" (used for the more common form "pathetically") which, while describing the manner of the crickets' action, brings in the response of the human observer: they end with a phenomenon which similarly concerns man's response to nature: the "Difference" that enhances the beauty of nature to the observer before the inevitable death of summer.

The poem contains two main vocabularies; one pertaining to nature, its landscape, inmates, and seasons: *Summer— Birds— Grass— Noon— August— Furrow—Glow—Nature.* This is a "native" and quite concrete diction. Religion affords the other set of words: *celebrates— Mass— Ordinance— Grace— Canticle—Repose—Druidic.* "Mass" and "Canticle" are terms used specifically in the Roman Catholic Church; "Ordinance" is principally a Protestant concept; and "Druidic" refers to a Pre-Christian religion. These terms belong to an abstract vocabulary of mixed heritage. The observer's reaction to the mass she is overhearing is first suggested in "pathetic," which to begin with may mean no more than "moving", but which acquires an element of sadness when perceived in the context of the entire poem. The adjective "pensive" strengthens the note of melancholy. The words "unobtrusive," "gradual," and "Custom" are counterpointed to "pathetic" and "pensive" as representing something more neutral and non-emotive: they help to control the expression of the emotion which the crickets' sounds evoke in the listener. Thus we are imperceptibly being prepared for a disclosure of the observer's response to the scene. In spite of this, we are startled by the nakedness and directness of the word "Loneliness" which appears exactly in the middle of the poem—it alone in the second stanza being an Anglo-Saxon noun among naturalized or Latinate words.

The words "gradual" and "Custom" which both relate to time lead up to "antiquest". This Dickinsonian superlative creates a problem for the explicator. What is its antecedent? Mass? Grace? or Loneliness? In the longer version of this poem Emily Dickinson writes "'Tis audibler at dusk"; she is apparently referring to the Mass. Since in the semi-final draft of the shorter version she first wrote "Antiquer", one might reasonably conclude that at least in its original form this word applied to the sounds heard. Elsewhere the poet links crickets to the concept of the ancient: "The Cricket spoke so clear / Presumption was—His Ancestors / Inherited the Floor—" (No. 1540 variant). In the final version of "Further in Summer than the Birds," the original reference may have become subsumed in the relation to the more emotionally charged and more immediate word "Loneliness". It is likely that in its vague reference "antiquest"—meaning "most ancient" or what we would call "most archetypal"—ties together the Mass, that is, the *cause* of the observer's thoughts and emotions: the Grace, which is the *influence* on the listener of the sounds overheard; and the Loneliness, which is the *result* of this influence.

"Noon," that is, the height of the day which in Dickinson's imagery stands for glory and fullfillment, contrasts (in what I would call a "slant" contrast) with the other time reference in the third stanza: "August burning low"; she uses the image of the candle or the lamp to indicate the time of year. These opposites crystallize the paradox of that moment when nature's beauty at its peak is about to fall off. Grammatical analysis will clarify the syntax of this stanza and the next. Inversion, ellipsis, and parenthesis obscure the structure and the meaning. The following would be a possible prose version: "It [The Loneliness?] is felt to be most antique at noon when—August burning low [i.e. nearing its end] this spectral canticle arises, typifying repose. As yet no grace has been remitted [i.e. no wrinkle mars the smoothness and brightness of the face of nature]." ("Grace" is used in its aesthetic sense as a contrast to ugliness and imperfection also in No. 355: "Deformed Men—ponder Grace—". "Glow" also represents life, as in No. 1384: "Praise it—'tis dead—/ It cannot glow—".)

In the final lines "Druidic" is the last link in the religious vocabulary. In it ends also the line from "antiquest" as a concept connected to a Pre-Christian period. It echoes the intangible and the mysterious, represented by the statement that "No Ordinance be seen," by the words "gradual Grace," and the adjectives "pensive" and "spectral," "Enhances," finally, looks back to "enlarging" of similar meaning, one referring to the beauty of nature, the other to the emotion that is caused in the human observer by the processes of nature.

The subject of this poem is easily stated: its theme and meaning are more elusive. In fact, its theme seems not one, but rather a complex of ideas. The metaphor of the mass and the references to loneliness have to be closely scrutinized to yield a maximum of meaning. What sort of mass is being celebrated? and why the loneliness? loneliness for what or whom? Richard Chase, who has given us some profound observations on this poem and the complex of ideas it represents, thinks that the mass is a requiem. I interpret it in a similar way, and I find support for this explication especially in the third stanza. A *canticle* is, according to the dictionary (*Webster*), specifically one of the biblical hymns or songs of praise used in church services. One of these is the *Nunc Dimittis* which begins with the words of Simeon, "Lord, now lettest thou thy servant depart in peace." The connotation of a death mass is reinforced by the following *repose* which means repose in the grave. The canticle *typifies*, that is, foreshadows death. An element of prophesying links the words "Canticle" and "typify" to the epithet "Druidic". It is the Druid as soothsayer that is preeminent in the idea of the "Druidic" change that is imminent. The Pre-Christian religion may also be more closely associated with nature than is Christianity. Elsewhere (No. 1115) the poet uses the word "prophetic" of some insects which presumably are crickets. In her wisdom, this poem says, nature sends "Appropriate Creatures" to announce her every change; she sends the crickets to prophesy about winter, the death of beauty and life.

Emily Dickinson seems to have been acutely sensitive to nature as something to be enjoyed and as an emblem of life and death. She testifies to this sensitivity in a letter to Higginson (June 7, 1862). She is speaking of her friend Benjamin Newton's death and of how her poetry is a relief to her:

And when far afterward—a sudden light on Orchards, or a new fashion in the wind troubled my attention—I felt a palsy,—here the Verses just relieve—

She feels a palsy this time; at another time what she experiences may be a feeling of loneliness. This loneliness is no doubt a sense of isolation: she observes nature, but is not permitted to participate in its processes or commune with it. Nature is indifferent to man: "Summer does not care", she says in another poem (No. 1386). It is also a sense of bereavement through death (cf. Nos. 903 and 1493). Paradoxically loneliness may enrich the one who feels it (cf. No. 1116).

In "Further in Summer than the Birds" Emily Dickinson does not commit herself as to the question of immortality. Death is referred to with ambivalence: *grace—antiquest—repose,* these words have no ugly or disagreeable connotations in the context of the poem. Still the new state which is imminent will involve a diminution of beauty, there will be furrows on the glow. The paradox is that the premonition of repose—a desirable state—makes us sorrowful and lonely. God is notably absent in the poem. We are indirectly reminded of His existence through the religious diction and imagery; but the poem's human observer does not commune with Him. Emily Dickinson was evidently aware that her poem expressed no hope of immortality, for in a letter accompanying the 1883 copy she writes: "I bring you a chill Gift— ... "

There remains to be commented on the word "Grace" as it is used in this poem about the influence of the crickets' song upon the listener. Being part of the metaphor of the mass, it conveys a sense of divine influence acting in man to purify him and make him morally strong. In my reading, this word takes on the meaning of *insight* and *wisdom.* It is an insight into the processes that nature and man undergo: and it discloses to us our plight as being isolated from both nature and God. In the poem "The Crickets sang" (No. 1104), the speaker recalls that moment of a late-summer evening when the crickets' song revealed to her "A Wisdom, without Face, or Name". In "Further in Summer than the Birds" the poet attempts to express an insight won that has no name, that is inexpressible in ordinary terms. But it can be conveyed, indeed it *has* been conveyed to us as imperceptibly as the grace spoken of in the poem. Emily Dickinson has successfully made her raid on the inarticulate.

From *The Voice of the Poet: Aspects of Style in the Poetry of Emily Dickinson* (Cambridge: Harvard Univ. Press, 1968), pp. 261-68.

WILLIAM ROSSKY

"A Clock stopped"

A Clock stopped—
Not the Mantel's—
Geneva's farthest skill
Cant put the puppet bowing—
That just now dangled still—

An awe came on the Trinket!
The Figures hunched, with pain—
Then quivered out of Decimals—
Into Degreeless Noon—

It will not stir for Doctor's—
This Pendulum of snow—
The Shopman importunes it—
While cool—concernless No—

Nods from the Gilded pointers—
Nods from the Seconds slim—
Decades of Arrogance between
The Dial life—,
And Him—

IN *Emily Dickinson's Poetry: Stairway of Surprise* (Holt, Rinehart & Winston, 1960), C. R. Anderson offers the most complete explication yet of "A Clock Stopped"; but, when he discusses principally the ways in which the imagery evokes the sense of physical death, I think he makes the poem seem static, misses the steady emotional development, and comes therefore, partly on grounds that "Him" must refer to God or to the soul of the dead, to the somewhat inexact conclusion that the poem ends with hints of immortality.

Stanza 1, with its sharp contrast of the recently active "bowing" to the stillness of the corpse, evokes a sense of sudden immobility in death, but, chiefly through the emphatically placed "*dangled* still" (my italics), conveys even more precisely the sudden limpness, the loss of the tension and tone of life. Stanza 2, returning briefly to the moment before death, now emphasizes the finality in the immobility of death, its absoluteness. First, in the context of the spasm of line 7, the "awe" that comes "on the Trinket" suggests the stricken aspect of the dying person rather than some specific reason for the awe, such as a glimpse of God or Heaven. But the ambiguity concerning the cause of awe prepares for a major idea in the poem—the impossibility of our knowing the reality of death itself. (Is the appearance of awe merely a physical phenomenon or does the dying person perceive some hidden immensity?) Then the stiff spasms of the moment become fixed in death. By final position and by meaning, "Degreeless Noon" stresses the feeling of absolute and eternal immobility. The two hands, stuck at noon, "Degreeless," can never move on; for, as Anderson sees, only if a second hand moves can an angle of "degree" appear. "Degreeless," then, is forever motionless, and the very singleness of the two hands at noon strengthens the sense of fixedness. Because of this feeling of permanent fixedness, the sense of immobility in stanza 2 seems even more intense than in 1. In stanza 3 not only is the immobility of the corpse, a frozen "Pendulum," further intensified, but the complete unresponsiveness of death, an effect developing naturally out of the perception of the very immobility, is also strongly evoked: to the importuning of the living, "Shopman" and "Doctor's," the unresponsive corpse gives a clear, indifferent "No." So strong is the unresponsiveness that, accented at the end of the third stanza, "No" pours over into the last: so strong is it that the utterly motionless, the still, has the force of action: it "Nods." Even if we accept with Anderson the reading "Stares" for "Nods" in line 14, this sense of the unresponsiveness of the corpse is not altered and, for that matter, the paradox of almost active unresponsiveness is still conveyed by "Nods" in line 15. Now, out of that unresponsiveness, arises in the last three lines of the poem a final awareness of the utter impenetrability of death, the terrible and frustrating yet inevitable mystery of death to the living. Between the living "Him" and the "still," unresponsive "Dial life" are unbridgeable, impossible "Decades of Arrogance." (Anderson's argument that "Him" cannot refer to "Shopman" or "Doctor" because "they are both on the same side of death as the stopped clock, the mortal side," does not hold; for "they" are "on the side" of life, as the corpse obviously is not.) The living cannot reach the dead nor, hence, the reality of death: the unresponsiveness of the corpse becomes a wall underscoring the complete impossibility of our knowing the answer to the mystery of death. Moreover the word "Arrogance" not only carries forward the sense of indifference in "cool—concernless" but also conveys a sense of conscious superiority. Both suggestions in the word help to accent the separation between living and dead—and even insinuate, perhaps, the superior knowledge of death which only the inscrutable dead and not the living can possess. Having moved from "dangled still" to the fixed immobility and then to the absolute unresponsiveness and thus to the impenetrability of death, we are left at the end responding to the awful mystery.

From "Dickinson's 'A Clock stopped,' " *The Explicator,* 22 (1963), Item 3.

JOHN CODY, M.D.

"The Soul has Bandaged moments"

OF THE crisis of 1857-1864 three main phases can be distinguished. The poet clearly recognized them herself as in the poem beginning "the Soul has Bandaged moments" to be referred to later. Her own designations for them exactly parallel the technical ones. In prosaic terminology there were the phases of (1) ego breakdown, (2) manic restitution, (3) constrictive reorganization, or in the poet's terms, the Soul's (1) bandaged moments, (2) moments of escape, (3) retaken moments.

In the stage of *ego breakdown* the poet experienced an inundation of uncontrolled erotic and hostile impulses escaping from repression and she feared that she was going mad. This stage was ushered in by the collapse of her unconscious hopes of fulfillment in her brother's marriage.

In the state of *manic restitution* the inadmissible impulses toward Austin and Sue were projected and displaced upon a less interdicted love object—the unattainable "beloved"—thereby reducing the fear and guilt and allowing a channeled expression of these feelings through the poetry.

In the stage of *constrictive reorganization* came the realization that this solution was also illusory and doomed to frustration. The agitation and exuberance of the previous stage were then replaced by depression, guilt feelings, over-control of all impulses and repudiation of the instinctual life. The creative drive, hampered by inhibitions and obsessive doubting, fell away.

The clarity with which Emily Dickinson perceived and recorded these changes in herself seems almost miraculous. The following poem contains all that has been inferred, and much more, about the morphology of her illness:

> The Soul has Bandaged moments—
> When too appalled to stir—
> She feels some ghastly Fright come up
> And stop to look at her—

Ego breakdown

> Salute her—with long fingers—
> Caress her freezing hair—
> Sip, Goblin, from the very lips
> The Lover—hovered—o'er—
> Unworthy, that a thought so mean
> Accost a Theme—so—fair—

The soul has moments of Escape—
When bursting all the doors—
She dances like a Bomb, abroad,
And swings upon the Hours,

Manic restitution

As do the Bee—delirious borne—
Long Dungeoned from his Rose—
Touch liberty—then know no more,
But Noon, and Paradise—

Constrictive reorganization

The Soul's retaken moments—
When, Felon led along,
With shackles on the plumed feet,
And staples, in the Song,

The Horror welcomes her again.
These are not brayed of Tongue.

For Soul, we may substitute Ego.

The Soul is bandaged—therefore *wounded,* kept from bleeding (losing integrity and ability to contain impulses) by flimsy gauze dressings (ego defenses). The Soul is too frightened to stir (catatonic rigidity). The "Fright" represents the escape of repressed impulses, seen to be erotic in the caressing and kissing, and hostile in their degradation of a "Theme so fair" (the marriage of Austin?).

In the middle part of the poem the impulses and the ego are participating in an uneasy relationship. The ego is highly energized and barely able to contain the impulses within safe channels of expression. The doors are burst (inhibitions swept away), the Soul dances (libidinous motoric release) "like a Bomb" (invested with destructive potentialities). As the Bee to his Rose, the Soul is borne "delirious" (heedless of reality) toward "Noon and Paradise" (sexual consummation).

In the final part, the Soul's flight is over, the plumed feet are shackled (depression, acceptance of the strictures of reality). The Soul is a "Felon" (oppressed with a sense of guilt) being led to imprisonment (the years of seclusion) and the song is stapled (the creative drive is bound and immobilized by inhibition).

That these three phases were not entirely separate and distinct but tended in reality to interpenetrate and alternate with each other is evident from the letters and the sequence of the poems. The fact is stated outright in this poem's penultimate line: "The Horror welcomes her again," which tells us that for some time after the poet retreated indoors the repressed fears and desires continued to threaten her sanity.[1]

1. Clark Griffith in *The Long Shadow, Emily Dickinson's Tragic Poetry*, pp. 216-219, gives an interpretation of this poem as a spiritual allegory of Emily Dickinson's relationship with God. It may be that what he has to say about the poem is closer to the poet's conscious intentions than the present interpretation. Nevertheless, if one equates evil with the repressed the two versions

When Emily Dickinson returned to her home in 1865, nevermore to leave it, she began to dress exclusively in white and never afterward departed from this custom. White she associated with marble, alabaster and frost—all her symbols of death.[2] White also symbolizes purity and virginity and it is the color of brides. Emily Dickinson felt herself a bride, "the wife without the sign . . . Empress of Calvary!"

. . . .

Late in the poet's life there occurred an illusion of emotional fulfillment resembling an echo or a mirage. The reference is not to her twilight affection for Judge Lord, whose love reawakened all her old sexual conflicts. Nor was it her love for Susan's tragic little boy Gilbert, who died in his eighth year. It involved Emily Dickinson and her mother.

One year to the day after the death of Emily's father, her mother, then 71, suffered a stroke and became paralyzed. Until her death over seven years later, she rested in a chair or lay in bed, a helpless invalid with wandering mind, unable to so much as lift a glass of water to her lips. After three years of this, she suffered a fractured hip, despite which she survived four more years, a continuous nursing care. Her nurses were her daughters, who tended her faithfully from morning till night.

During that long illness the estrangement of the years seemed to dissolve and Emily, to her astonishment, experienced something very like the love she had sought so long. She wrote of her deep sense of loss at her mother's death: "As we bore her dear form through the Wilderness, Light seemed to have stopped."

Later she explained, "We were never intimate mother and children when she was our Mother but Mines in the same ground meet by tunnelling and when she became our child, the affection came."

The "affection came" because the identification of daughter with mother, so long delayed and so tragically, at last became possible. With the reversal of roles the daughter became the mother, the mother the helpless child. In her daily ministrations Emily suddenly became aware of a source within herself from which she was enabled to pour forth upon her "child" quantities of devotion. And in the process she recovered, through the reflection back upon herself of this, her own newly awakened maternal tenderness, the "Dominions" that had so long been "lost."

From "Mourner Among the Children," *Psychiatric Quarterly*, 41 (1967), 12-37: 233-61.

---

are compatible though on different psychic levels.

2. Although there is no biographical support for such an interpretation it is possible that the inner upheaval of the preceding years induced a premature psychogenic menopause. The symbolism of white garments being multipally determined, might unconsciously express this without negating other interpretations. The wearing of white camellias to signify the absence of menses is well known from the novel *Camille* and the opera *"La Traviata."*

Evaluations

HENRY W. WELLS

The Exact Word

EMILY DICKINSON is one of the foremost masters of poetic English since Shakespeare, and in the severe economy of her speech comparable to Dante. Fascinating as the meaning or ideas in her poetry may be, and important as are her metaphors, verse architecture, rhythm, and euphony, it is her study of the individual word and her masterly discovery of the right word that chiefly defines her distinction. Although a word may be rich in metaphorical implications, and strictly in its rightful place in the architecture of sense and harmony of sound, it is of the word in itself that Emily apparently thought first and it is of language as built out of individual words that we ourselves chiefly think in analyzing her poetry. Emily was a worshipper of atoms, and the atoms from which her imaginative world was built were verbal. Happily, abundant proof exists of her devotion to language. The misfortune that her poems were long delayed in publication is more than cancelled by the good fortune that they now exist in copious manuscripts, some of which have already been reproduced in facsimile. These manuscripts give conclusive evidence, were any such external evidence required, of her verbal-mindedness. It became her custom to weigh words with the utmost meticulousness, sometimes writing nine or ten in the place of one to scrutinize more closely which should be preferred. Her manuscripts present some of the most amazing records of scrupulous rewriting recorded in literary history. She clearly thought even more diligently of the individual words than of any other feature of a poem. This mistress of lyrical spontaneity became also a miser of syllables, an indefatigable judge and critic of her vocabulary. Her readers do well to approach her poetry in the same spirit, viewing each poem as a medallion in the vast design of her literary creation, and each medallion as a mosaic of words like precious stones, fastidiously chosen.

Emily lived in a world of love, scorn, stars, flowers, brightness, and menacing night, where it was her one constant faith that with due labor she could always find a word for every object and every experience. If on some occasion this proved impossible, as noted in her poem, "I found a phrase to every thought I ever had, but one", the exception constituted a mere freak, curious but thoroughly unimportant. The important truth was her wholly confirmed belief in the efficacy of words. She never complains of their vagueness. Nature, she declares, did at times betray her, as it betrays all men. But she records no snake in the garden of language. Speech was something God-given, potentially errorless. What faults there were in actuality lay with the speakers. Such was her almost platonic devotion and love, not toward mankind, but toward the language of poetry.

In one of her most important aphorisms she declares that the lip would crumble could the mind conceive "the undeveloped freight of a delivered syllable." Nothing could better express her reverence for the power of words. They were to her like particles of radium, infinite power within an almost invisible substance; like the potent grains of sand envisaged by William Blake. One of her briefest poems, "A word is dead", is dedicated to the thought that the statement in its first line is an error amounting to gross atheism. Emily concludes that the word properly spoken is alive; indeed she knows nothing more tremblingly, more vibrantly alive. Had she placed more faith in the revelations of the orthodox creed, she might well have found esoteric meanings in the opening verses of the Gospel of Saint John: "In the beginning was the word". Her life became a long laboratory study of words, a laboratory of genuine experimentation, and not a mere museum. Her library, however important, was always secondary to her practice. The created word, which she sometimes called the spoken word, to her signified considerably more than the word as read. Yet more than passing notice must be taken of her researches in language. Her early love affair, some say, was with a tutor who instructed her in the mysteries of literature and vocabulary, and who left her on his premature death a devoted student of her dictionary. The dictionary was the bible of her religion, which was poetry. Her personal dictionary was Noah Webster's, the illustrious philologist who had for a time lived in the town of Amherst, laid the cornerstone of one of the buildings of Amherst College, of which her father was trustee, and left his powerful mark on the thinking of the community. The dictionary was the mine from which the gold of poetry was to be extracted, and several references to mines in her own poems show with what an awe she regarded mines. The dictionary she came to consider the one book more an essential than any other for the writing of her own poems. Yet naturally she revered her predecessors in poetry, who had so conclusively proved what words could achieve. Two books which she probably regarded as almost equally poetical, undoubtedly in her mind surpassed all others as guiding and inspirational forces for her style. These, conservatively and almost inevitably enough, were the Bible and Shakespeare. Truly as her style is her own, it becomes evident that from these sources she won much of her sagacity in language. From the Bible she received encouragement in forthright, dignified, simple, and earnest statement; from Shakespeare she gained encouragement for the bolder flights of her imagination and fancy, for her large vocabulary, her audacious use of the parts of speech, and, occasionally, her more than Asiatic opulence. Nevertheless the most fruitful commentary on her style certainly does not lie in comments on her "influences." These are incidental. With Emily it becomes necessary to start afresh.

The starting point is undoubtedly the pointedness with which she employs the individual word. Each principal word in a major lyric constitutes for her the equivalent of a universe. Some writers never use one word where they may use ten, she never uses two where she can use one. Her rejected words would fill a volume many times larger than her actual works. It hardly becomes hyperbole to say that a single word in her poetry often contains more imaginative energy than an entire lyric by a respectable but less distinguished poet. She seeks to give the word a poetic luminence over and beyond its literal connotation as defined by the dictionary, or its prosaic meanings in familiar conversation. To use a term common in her own writing, she aims to present each word in "italic". Such is her fruitful theory of poetry, or of the poetic style, which obviously comes to much the same thing.

An example will be helpful, and clearly hundreds present themselves with equal claims. One, quite arbitrarily chosen, serves to introduce the subject. A newly published poem begins:

> He lived the life of ambush
> And went the way of dusk.

Here the vital words are obviously those at the end of the lines, namely, "ambush", and "dusk". Their meanings are not specific, as are words in simple prose, but are poetically clear, emotionally and imaginatively powerful. Neither Emily nor anyone else will use these words again with quite these shades of value. They give us the feeling of vast oceanic reservoirs of experience. And this image in itself hints at a clue to Emily's style, which is, in brief, an ideal style for lyric poetry: her words resemble oceans, while those of less successful writers resemble lakes.

Before breaking down the subject into its parts through critical analysis, two or three more illustrations of Emily's uncanny felicity should be fruitful. One of her adjectives has often been remembered as evidence of her profound understanding of the New England climate. It will be recalled that she wrote, "There is a maritime conviction In the atmosphere". Observations of a lifetime are crammed here into a single epithet. Of course when her writing is at her best, this distinguished use of words is closely sustained, so that a sentence resembles a cluster of stars. In these lines she describes a neglected burying-ground:

> Strangers strolled and spelled
> At the lone orthography
> Of the elder dead.

The analysis of such a passage is necessarily somewhat personal. These are delicate, subjective matters, difficult of approach and beyond which it is impossible to go. Nevertheless I venture to think that many readers have been left almost breathless by the calm mastery, the high felicity, of the above lines. The words themselves are, of course, not rare, though "orthography" is hardly common. The point is that no one but Emily would have been likely to use them in just this way, with just this content. Other writers would in all probability have missed both her delicate feeling and its still more exquisite expression. They would have been satisfied, as Longfellow certainly would have been, with far easier statements. Others would, presumably, never have thought of "spelled", "lone", "orthography" or "elder"; they might even have missed "stranger", and "strolled". Emily misses nothing, or, in any case, no one is inspired enough to say what it is she misses.

Frequently her customary verse rhetoric reveals in brilliant light the italic emphasis placed upon individual words. Her manner curiously resembles that of a great poet whose style cannot well have been overly familiar to her, Dante. The poem, "Who never lost, are unprepared A coronet to find", ends with the statement that angels wrote the word, "Promoted" on a soldier's forehead. This type of supernatural inscription, preternaturally condensed, closely duplicates images many times repeated in the *Purgatorio*. Similarly, in the lyric, " 'Twas like a maelstrom", graphically describing a death agony, the action of the poetic narrative terminates when "A creature gasped 'Reprieve!' " One remembers death scenes as related in the *Purgatorio*. The Dantesque practice of concluding the sketch of a character with the name, thus giving the proper name the highest possible emphasis, is repeated in Emily Dickinson's elegy on her spiritual sister, Charlotte Brontë, where the word "Brontë" is studiously reserved for the last line. Similar art gives stress and poignancy to " 'I want', it pleaded all its life", a lyric wholly based upon the sharp contrast between the pre-emptory words, "I want" in the first line and the pathetic word, "Please", in the conclusion. How Emily's spirit dwelt upon the overpowering force of single words is further hinted in her notable lyric, "I never hear the word 'escape' Without a quicker blood". The entire poem hinges on this living word, a spark kindling a considerable blaze.

The remarkable brevity of her poems in itself lends emphasis to each word. To this condition should be added her obvious dislike for the small change of language. Her style on occasions becomes almost crabbed through bold dispensing with articles, to be seen, for example, in the phrase, "As unto crowd". If she uses long or rare words, she has good reason to do so, for she utterly avoids inflated rhetoric. In her worship of directness the Bible became her tutor. In *Genesis* it is sometimes written of one who died that he merely "was not". This terse phrase impressed Emily:

> "Was not" was all the statement.
> The unpretention stuns,
> Perhaps the comprehension;
> They wore no lexicons.

Her ideal of concision leads to a statement that might well be taken to summarize her own autobiographical poetry and the relation of her verse to her life.

> Its past set down before the soul,
> And lighted with a match,
> Perusal to facilitate
> Of its condensed despatch.

The poems, and even the individual words, resemble match flames lighted to illuminate a crucial moment of the soul. Success depends almost wholly on condensation of expression. Each poem becomes a telegram from "infinity".

Often in the first or last lines of her poems there appears a word peculiarly illumined with such a supernatural brightness. "Glee! the great storm is over!" begins one of her dramatic lyrics, with evidence of her command over one of the rarer and more recalcitrant parts of speech, the exclamation. "To fight *aloud* is very brave", begins a poem contrasting bravery in battle or in the active world with spiritual courage. The meditative poem commencing, "I found the phrase to every thought", accents in its last phrases the unusual words "cochineal", and "mazarin". The brilliant, "I know that he exists", proceeds from its lukewarm and orthodox beginning to an amazingly vigorous and imaginative close, inquiring if God's jest has not "crawled" too far. Special attention is challenged by the language of the initial lines: "Softened by Time's consummate plush"; "An awful tempest mashed the air"; "The overtakelessness of death"; and "The silver reticence of death".

That the true wealth of language often depends on a frugality of syllables appears in striking passages composed wholly in monosyllables. This is Emily's monolithic style, witnessed in such expression as, "Should the glee glaze In death's stiff stare". The simplest word may prove the most potent. Thus in the harrowingly realistic little elegy, "A clock stopped—not the mantel's", the word "No" receives extreme accent, being the rhyme word at the end of a stanza and carrying on the meaning of the sentence unbroken into the stanza following. What a "No" is there! The dictionary defines no such vibrant negative. She delights in common expressions, as when, it will be remembered, she calls Elijah's chariot by no other name than a wagon. The understatement, so long a practice in Anglo-Saxon verse and further advanced by Puritan reticence and humor, also came most naturally to Emily and materially aided in the creation of her style. A good example occurs in one of the grimmest of her works, an account of drowning: "The water chased him as he fled". The lines describe the "revolting bliss" promised by some demon billow of the sea. But drowning was not really a pleasure, as harsh fact proved. The little poem ends with the menacing lines: "The object floating at his side Made no distinct reply." The particular "object" Emily in leaving undefined makes all the more terrifying. These are the devious ways of poetry.

As the last quotation indicates, the poetic word or phrase is distinguished from the non-poetic in that the former is rich in implications, a truism whose implications are themselves too seldom regarded. Poetic words are suggestive. This primary requirement of her art Emily grasps fully. "Except the heaven had come so near", begins one of her lyrics. Presumably the poem is a love poem, but denoting a love of what or whom? For what does the word "heaven" stand? The artist, like nature, preserves mysterious taciturnity.

. . . .

Although most of Emily's words are sufficiently common, she employs a large vocabulary including many rare words and some of her own manufacture. When she writes that butterflies "Leap, plashless, as they swim", a rare usage becomes apparent. She finds the the exact use for such an unusual word as "omnifold". A deliberate and significant quaintness is cast upon her thought by such terms as "farness" and "foreignhood". She avails herself of Shakesperean license. Indeed she unobtrusively borrows from Shakespeare. It was probably the great dramatist who suggested to her the frequent interchange of parts of speech and the bold formation of vivid verbs. In a passage rich in Shakesperean images she uses the verb "beggars", borrowed presumably from the same form in one of her favorite plays, *Antony and Cleopatra*.

Her language, then is highly uncommon and poetic in that she employs familiar words in unfamiliar phrases. It suits her purpose to call mountains, "purple territories", to write of noon as "the parlor of the day", to address angels familiarly as "sapphire fellows", to speak of a "fleshless chant", and a "seamless company", to use "orchestra" as a verb, to speak of frost as a "blond assassin", to tell of the "gnash" of northern winds, to speak of a "pile" of wind, to use "became" in place of the less vigorous verb to be, to speak of "narrow" time, to coin the adverb "russetly", to write of a flower's "unobtrusive" face, as "punctuating" a wall, to relate the star's "Etruscan argument", to address the "staunch" dust, humorously to call hell "the Phosphorus of God", to use "again" and "until" as nouns, to write of "alabaster zest", of "sumptuous" destitution, of "sequestration" from decay, and of "phlegmatic" mountains.

Each of these words as employed by Emily Dickinson is a highly vigorous creative act, each in itself a poem. In mythology are many legends to the effect that each drop of a hero's blood comes to life. Emily's words are drops of her heart's blood. Each stands up a hero active in the triumphant wars of the spirit, armed with bow of burning gold and arrow of desire. Thus analysis of her language reduces her art to its lowest denominator, discovering it thoroughly alive and thoroughly sound. Examination can go no further, for it is a poet's ultimate claim to be a master of words ever employed in the service of the spirit of Man.

From Henry W. Wells, *Introduction to Emily Dickinson* (Chicago: Packard, 1947), pp. 276-86.

RICHARD CHASE

Poetic Themes

IN EMILY DICKINSON'S poetry, taking it by and large, there is but one major theme, one symbolic act, one incandescent center of meaning. Expressed in the most general terms, this theme is the achievement of status through crucial experiences. The kinds of status our poet imagines are variously indicated by such favorite words as "queen," "royal," "wife," "woman," "poet," "immortal," and "empress." The kinds of experience which confer status are love, "marriage," death, poetic expression, and immediate intuitive experiences which have the redemptive power of grace. We have here the basis of a fairly complex and various poetry. Yet we must observe that the view of life which our poet has taken for her central theme is based even more severely than it at first seems on a series of sharp and definitive exclusions. Each "estate" involves its own renunciation, except·for one: immortality. And each of the crucial experiences which confer the different kinds of status is a type and emblem of one of them: the coming of death.

This is not to imply, of course, that she has no topic but death and immortality. But it remains true that we cannot see her work very clearly until we perceive that her best and most characteristic poems proliferate from one center of energy and that many of her lesser poems either try to issue from this center and fail or else do not issue from any center at all and remain random gnomic observations or incidental experiments and notations. The fact that many of these random observations display great charm, wit, and even the visionary power of genius should not lead us to blur the edges of her fine power of self-limitation. We know life mostly by thirsting for it, as she repeatedly states. And we know freedom largely by being prisoners. To slake the thirst with too much wine, to enfranchise the prisoner too abruptly or too completely is to invite surfeit and extinction. These are not the sentiments of a freely ranging and widely various mind. They are the sentiments of a mind which instinctively inclines to its characteristic bias.

"Experience" in Emily Dickinson's best poetry is narrow and profound. Typically it takes the form of a sudden illumination, an appalling pause in the motion of things, a seizure of an unspeakable power, an ecstatic influx. Her favorite images for the typical experience are a bolt of lightning, a brilliant light, the sun, the eruption of a volcano, the unannounced arrival of a lover in his coach, the surprising knock of his hand upon the door, the confrontation of some threatening or overwhelming natural or psychic phenomenon. Experience at its lower and less decisive intensity tends to be the reverberation, the afterglow, or the diminishing memory of the few forcibly revelatory experiences. This is the warrant for her fanciful idea of the simultaneity of experience—for her idea, to take one example, that she was

> Born—Bridalled—
> Shrouded—
> In a day.

It is her warrant for assuming the typicality of experience, an assumption which leads her to the sometimes questionable conclusion that she perfectly knows what it is to be married or to die.

When she speaks specifically of experience as if all limitations might be easily transgressed, she leaves the privilege to God. For God, each morning may be new, unique: "the Experiment of our Lord." But if we consider the possibilities of experience open to human beings we merely gain a new sense of its closure. In "Experience is the angled road" she calls it a testimony to the "complicate" discipline of man that experience always compels him to choose "his pre-appointed plan."

If we assume from such a poem as "Water is taught by thirst" that Emily Dickinson is propounding an open universe in which knowledge is freely derivable in the pragmatic or empirical manner, we are brought up short by the realization that, according to this poem, everything man learns from is represented by some emblem of disintegration or death: thirst, oceans (usually a symbol of eternity in her poems), throe, battles, memorial mold, and snow.

And if we assume that this poem, and the several others which deal with opposites like "water" and "thirst," is evidence of a widely ranging system of tensions or of a dialectical cast of mind, we are investing Emily Dickinson's work with meanings it does not have. She has, as we shall note, an admirable vein of "Stoicism." But this does not mean, as some writers have seemed to think, that she produced a philosophy of tensions. She had certain visionary qualities in common with Blake, and she invented a poetically imagined eschatology. But this is no evidence that she developed a dialectic of contraries.

An "experience" means an emptiness newly filled or informed or enlivened—or a fullness made empty. One of the aphorisms of her letters reads: "Nature is a haunted house, but art, a house that tries to be haunted." And she distinguishes from nature in this respect not only art but human existence itself. One may discern two sources for this idea of experience. The first is the Puritan tradition, with its characteristic notion of grace. As Perry Miller says: "Regeneration was the receiving by man of 'the fulnesse of the infinitenesse of all perfections which are in the Lord,' who alone is 'able to fill up all the empty chinks, void places, the unsatisfied graspings & yawnings of the spirit of man. . . . ' Therefore grace is to be understood as something inward and spiritual, and when it has wrought upon a man in regeneration 'it leaves an impression upon the most inward motions of the soul, as they meet with God in the most retired and refined actions thereof.'" In Emily Dickinson's accounts of how her spirit yearns for the fulness of infinity and of how it is "fathomed" by the emanations of a mysterious power she remains a true daughter of her New England ancestors.

The second source of her idea of experience is simply her reaction to the culture of provincial America. Tocqueville, after delineating the emptiness, the monotony, and tenuousness of this culture, predicted that American poetry would derive a mythology of universalism and abstraction from its cultural habitat. His prediction was amply justified by the appearance of Walt Whitman. He neglected to imagine the appearance of such writers as Hawthorne and Melville and Emily Dickinson, who were more interested in the haunting of the house than in singing the song of the open road. For these writers existence was an emptiness to be filled by the imagination.

It has often been remarked that American, and particularly New England, writers have to be read in the light of their relation to experience. Experience, that is, has been a problem, something to conjure with, to American writers as it has not typically been for Europeans. The particular qualities of experience could not be assumed among Americans as known and identifiable, because of the newness of the New World and because of the Puritan ideas of sin and renunciation which, in conduct if not always in theory, placed the individual in opposition to his experience and forced him to question it. Emily Dickinson shares this American tendency of opposing the individual to his experience. But her idea of what experience is differentiates her from some writers and puts her in the company of others.

She differs from Emerson in the separations she makes. Emerson is often tempted to assert a too easy correspondence between man, cosmos, and God, and too easy interflux of consciousness, nature, and spirit. But experience for Emily Dickinson is not the act of dilating and expanding into harmony with a loosely conceived cosmos or deity. It is the dramatic action of one thing upon another, the influx of power or illumination from nature or God which is received by something radically different from either, man.

She has moments remotely reminiscent of Whitmanesque intoxication and singing of oneself. But Whitman's myriad perceptions of natural experience were certainly beyond her, and one may well conclude that she and not Whitman gains by the contrast. Whitman's mind, despite the voracious setting down of facts, was strongly transcendental and abstract. Emily Dickinson's grasp upon reality was narrower, but within its limits it could often be a good deal more firm.

Among the romantic poets of the early part of the century, her mind was perhaps closest to Wordsworth's. But the closeness is not very marked, consisting largely in the formal coincidence that both poets tend to subsume experience under the revelatory moments when the "gleam," to use Wordsworth's term, suffuses the mind and to stress the importance of memory, whose function it is to recapture and retain the experience of the "gleam." But Emily Dickinson expresses, for example, no idea of the development of man from childhood to maturity of the kind one finds in Wordsworth, and for her the revelation of truth through experience has a much more abrupt and definitive quality, in the Puritan manner, than it has for the English poet. Again she sees no such correspondence of mind with nature as does Wordsworth. She differs from most romantic poets and from the American Transcendentalists because, as she sees it, nature not only fails to give daily support to the life and reason of man but actively threatens him with extinction.

The rather stark simplifications of Emily Dickinson's view of human experience rule out the possibility that she should develop a complex or subtle psychology. In this respect she is like Hawthorne rather than Wordsworth or Melville. Reality and truth have for Emily Dickinson and Hawthorne so much the quality of something finally given to the clairvoyant mind once and for all that they do not easily take to ideas of evolution and unfolding. Wordsworth may trace the development of man's personality with the greatest scrupulosity and ingenuity. Melville may delineate in the figures of legend the gradual emergence of his Ishmael. But for Hawthorne and Emily Dickinson reality tends to appear hard and fast, emblematic and typical. Truth is given, not evolved.

From *Emily Dickinson* (New York: William Sloane, 1951), pp. 121-27.

THEODORA WARD

Death and Immortality

THE DISSOLVING world in which Emily now found herself brought her within two years into a position that is seldom reached at her age by those who live in the ever shifting circles of a broader environment. It is probable that a lifelong physical weakness began at this time to develop into the disease that brought about her death two years later, but in the finer adjustments of mind and body it is impossible to tell which is cause and which is effect. Death was now the medium through which she saw life. With the pervasion of a sense of finality there seems to have come no clear and steady vision of immortality such as sometimes illumines the last years of the aged. When at the time of Judge Lord's dangerous illness she had written to Washington Gladden, whose liberal preaching and writing had brought him into prominence, to ask if immortality were true, she was seeking help for herself, though she made her friend's peace of mind her excuse. After his death she made it clear in a letter to his friend Benjamin Kimball that he had found peace of mind in a different way.

> Perhaps to solidify his faith was for him impossible, and if for him, how more, for us! . . .
> Neither fearing Extinction, nor prizing Redemption, he believed alone. Victory was his Rendezvous—

While Dr. Wadsworth lived she leaned on the security of his faith when her own wavered, as she implied when she wrote to Charles Clark in October 1883:

> These thoughts disquiet me, and the great friend is gone, who could solace them. Do they disturb you?

> The Spirit lasts—but in what mode—
> Below, the Body speaks,
> But as the Spirit furnishes—
> Apart, it never talks—
> The Music in the Violin
> Does not emerge alone
> But Arm in Arm with Touch, yet Touch
> Alone—is not a Tune—

The Spirit lurks within the Flesh
Like Tides within the Sea
That make the Water live, estranged
What would the Either be?
Does that know—now—or does it cease—
That which to this is done,
Resuming at a mutual date
With every future one?
Instinct pursues the Adamant,
Exacting this Reply—
Adversity if it may be, or
Wild Prosperity,
The Rumor's Gate was shut so tight
Before my Mind was sown,
Not even a Prognostic's Push
Could make a Dent thereon—

The final quatrain, so forceful in its denial of the slightest possibility of finding
an answer to her questions that she used it in slightly variant form in three
separate poems, betrays the urgency of her search. She seemed to assume that
for Dr. Wadsworth himself the Heaven he believed in was realized at his death,
but closer to her own mind was Judge Lord's open uncertainty. The glimpses
of immortality she had been given all through her life in moments of ecstatic
insight from an unknown source had never become for her a solid foundation
for faith in conscious life after death. One of the last datable poems, left
unfinished, as if the thought itself were never completed, is in a mood of protest
against the inescapable, omnipresent concept of immortality.

Why should we hurry—why indeed
When every way we fly
We are molested equally
by immortality
no respite from the inference
that this which is begun
though where it's labors lie
A bland uncertainty
Besets the sight
This mighty night

The disjointedness of the last four lines, obviously jotted down for later testing,
and the force of the word "Tragedy," underlined twice, standing in the center
of the page, portray a mood in which the prospect of absolute extinction would
be preferable to the torment of the unknowable.

It need not be assumed, however, that Emily lived in an atmosphere of
gloom. On the contrary, when the ties that held her to life were cut one by
one, she seemed to find new freedom and detachment that brought added

meaning to the smallest events. She followed the happenings in the lives of friends and neighbors with as much concern as she had felt in earlier years, and in her letters to them was able to share their feelings and meet their moods, writing to each in the vein best suited to his age or type of mind. She never lost her joy in playing with words, and her sense of fun still lurked ready for provocation, even under grim circumstances. After a burglary had occurred at Austin's house in November 1885, the month that marked the beginning of her last long period of illness, she wrote to Ned, "Burglaries have become so frequent, is it quite safe to leave the Golden Rule out over night?" It was scarcely a month before she died that she gave her aunt Mrs. Currier an account of a local scandal, commenting, "Dont you think Fumigation ceased when Father died?"

There was even an intensification of perception in her last years, which she recognized when she wrote to Mrs. Holland late in 1884:

> All grows strangely emphatic, and I think if I should see you again, I sh'd begin every sentence with "I say unto you—" The Bible dealt with the Centre, not with the Circumference—

Everything was seen in the intensely clear light that sometimes occurs just after sundown. It is even possible that she came nearer than ever before to arresting the transitory ecstasy of which all her life she had received fleeting experiences. One of the last poems she completed gives ecstasy a place of supreme value in a world from which everything else had been taken away. It seems to have had great meaning for her at the time, for she incorporated it into letters to three friends during the year 1885, in which it appears as verse in letters to Mr. and Mrs. Loomis and to Helen Hunt Jackson, and as prose in a little note to Samuel Bowles the younger, each time given a different connotation.

> Take all away from me, but leave me Ecstasy,
> And I am richer then than all my Fellow Men—
> Ill it becometh me to dwell so wealthily
> When at my very Door are those possessing more
> In abject poverty—

Her business was no longer Circumference, but, as she said of the Bible, the Centre. Of immortality as a future state she was never sure, and human love was too vulnerable to loss to be relied on as a force with which to encounter death. Ecstasy, the gift of the gods, was the living flame at the center of the poet's own being. After all else was taken away she found the spark still burning. It was as a poet that she must take leave of life, sure of nothing except the unnamed meaning at the core of life itself.

From *The Capsule of the Mind: Chapters in the Life of Emily Dickinson* (Cambridge: Harvard Univ. Press, 1961), pp. 108-12.

HYATT H. WAGGONER

The Transcendent Self

IF HER only consistency was the consistency of growth, we ought to be able to say something about the direction of that growth, perhaps even discern its stages. Until recently, this was impossible, but now that we have all the letters and all the poems, most of them dated, we can at least make a start. But it will have to be a very tentative one, partly because I shall have to assume the correctness of Johnson's dating of letters and poems, but even more because the subject is large enough, and complex enough, for a book that has yet to be written. A "perhaps" should be understood as preceding all the major assertions in what follows.

Reading all the poems at one time, so that one has them more or less in mind all at once, has resulted, in this reader, in several preliminary impressions. Apart from the love poems and occasional poems—saying goodbye to a friend, writing a thank-you note in verse—the majority of her poems may be classified as relating to one of three subjects on which she carried on an inner debate. She debated with her father on the subject of the validity of his faith, she debated with Emerson on the validity of *his,* and she debated with both of them, her *two* fathers as it were, on the question of whether there could be any valid faith at all, as they both thought.

Logically, she had won the debate with her father at least as early as 1859, but the debate continued for many years, for her victory was of the mind only, not the heart, and she found herself drawn back again and again to questions she had already resolved. Some of her finest poems on this subject date from as late as the early seventies. Meanwhile the debate with Emerson had begun in the early sixties, at a time when personal crises made her feel that pain and limitation ought to be given a central place in any description of experience, not ignored or mentioned only as an afterthought in what she came to feel was Emerson's way. By 1875 she had made all the criticisms of Emerson's doctrines she was ever to make. "Unto the Whole—how add?" was so devastating a critique of the master's faith considered as a *religion* that it left nothing more to be said: and for once she *said* nothing more in this vein. Though some of her later poems might have been written by Emerson himself, they ignore the more metaphysical aspects of his doctrine. His somewhat pantheistic "Idealism" had ceased to be an issue for her.

The third subject of the inner dialogue recorded in her poems, the debate in which her skeptical self opposed both her fathers, began in the early sixties, reached its peak in the late sixties and early seventies, and then was dropped entirely. Among the poems dated by Johnson in the years from 1879 on until her death in 1886, not one of them returns to the question of whether *any* sort of religious faith is possible for one both informed and honest with himself. "Faith" in these last poems comes to be thought of as a "venture" of the soul with no expectation of "proof" from either a sacred Book or the sign language of nature. Whereas both her father and Emerson had thought that their very different faiths had rested on some sort of *revelation,* divine or natural, and would have agreed that without revelation there could *be* no faith, Dickinson came to believe that, far from being required by anything we could "know" about a reality outside ourselves, faith was simply a "first necessity" of our being, resting on nothing but need.

Redefining faith as commitment in the manner of later Existentialists was agonizingly difficult. Against both the fathers she had urged lack of evidence, an insufficiency of revelation. Increasingly in the sixties she had found God faceless and nature silent, until by 1868 she could announce, "That odd old man is dead a year," and in the following year anticipate Frost's "Design," with which this book began:

> A Spider sewed at Night
> Without a Light
> Upon an Arc of White.
> If Ruff it was of Dame
> Or Shroud of Gnome
> Himself himself inform.
> Of Immortality
> His Strategy
> Was Physiognomy.

In the same year she had written what is perhaps her most despairing poem, beginning "The Frost of Death was on the Pane" and concluding

> We hated Death and hated Life
> And nowhere was to go
> Than sea and continent there is
> A larger—it is Woe—.

It was out of such despair as this that her redefinition of faith came, and with it, a new acceptance of life as tragic but not necessarily meaningless. The new definition is best expressed in an early poem, written at a time when she already knew theoretically what her heart could not yet accept:

> Faith—is the Pierless Bridge
> Supporting what We see
> Unto the Scene that We do not—
> Too slender for the eye

It bears the Soul as bold
As it were rocked in Steel
With Arms of Steel at either side—
It joins—behind the Veil

To what, could We presume
The Bridge would cease to be
To our far, vacillating Feet
A first Necessity.

When in the years after 1879 she returned to the subject of the nature of faith itself, she reaffirmed the definition she had first achieved at a time when it could not help her. A little poem of 1881 will serve as an example of many similar ones:

Not seeing, still we know—
Not knowing, guess—
Not guessing, smile and hide
And half caress—
And quake—and turn away,
Seraphic fear—
Is Eden's innuendo
"If you dare"?

Her new "proveless" faith did not cancel anything she knew. It left her as aware as ever of "transport's instability" (contra Emerson), of the impossibility of imagining "costumeless consciousness" (contra her father and personal immortality), aware of what it meant to "cling to nowhere" waiting for the "Crash of nothing." Yet it did have two effects. More often now she returns to Emersonian sentiments like those of "A Route of Evanescence," which dates from this period. Emerson might have written

Estranged from Beauty—none can be—
For Beauty is Infinity—
And power to be finite ceased
Before Identity was leased.

Or this:

No matter where the Saints abide,
They make their Circuit fair
Behold how great a Firmament
Accompanies a Star.

The other effect was on the tone of her references to the Bible. Though she still thought it as a whole "an Antique Volume—/Written by faded Men/At the suggestion of Holy Spectres," more often now she wrote of Christ sympathetically—

> Obtaining but our own Extent
> In whatsoever Realm—
> 'Twas Christ's own personal Expanse
> That bore him from the Tomb—

or with gentle humor

> The Savior must have been
> A docile Gentleman—
> To come so far so cold a Day
> For little Fellowmen—
>
> The Road to Bethlehem
> Since He and I were Boys
> Was leveled, but for that 'twould be
> A rugged billion Miles—.

More often now the *example* of Christ seemed relevant to her:

> How brittle are the Piers
> On which our Faith doth tread—
> No Bridge below doth totter so—
> Yet none hath such a Crowd.
>
> It is as old as God—
> Indeed—'twas built by him—
> He sent his Son to test the Plank,
> And he pronounced it firm.

Her finest expression of what Christ had come to mean to her would probably have pleased even her father, if he had still been alive to read it and she had shown it to him:

> The Road was lit with Moon and star—
> The Trees were bright and still—
> Descried—by the distant Light
> A Traveller on a Hill
> To magic Perpendiculars
> Ascending, through Terrene—
> Unknown his shimmering ultimate—
> But he indorsed the sheen—

And he would certainly have agreed with the emphasis in the final lines of
one of her greatest poems of this period:

> Glass was the Street—in tinsel Peril
> Tree and Traveller stood—
> Filled was the Air with merry venture
> Hearty with Boys the Road—
>
> Shot the lithe Sleds like shod vibrations
> Emphasized and gone
> It is the Past's supreme italic
> Makes this Present mean—.

And so she arrived at the simple, almost doctrineless, but existentially
meaningful faith she expressed most succinctly two years before her death:

> Though the great Waters sleep,
> That they are still the Deep,
> We cannot doubt—
> No vacillating God
> Ignited this Abode
> To put it out—.

The development I have been tracing through the poems is perfectly apparent simply from an inspection of the poems themselves, without considering
any external evidence. But the letters tell the same story, often using some of
the same phrases. For instance, writing of the death of her mother some two
years before she wrote the poem just quoted, she says:

> She slipped from our fingers like a flake gathered by the wind, and
> is now part of the drift called "the infinite."
> We don't know where she is, though so many tell us.
> I believe we shall in some manner be cherished by our Maker—that
> the One who gave us this remarkable earth has the power still farther
> to surprise that which He has caused. Beyond that all is silence. . . .

Writing a friend at Christmas the same year (1882), to thank her for a
Christmas gift, she epitomizes most of what I have been saying about the
growth of her mind as I have traced it through the poems. This letter was
written when her own griefs and losses were piling up faster and faster, when
her own health was precarious and her death not far off, but in it we may see
the familiar dialogic play of a keen and restless mind, the familiar valor, the
old gallant attempt to strengthen another perhaps less strong, the old movement of the mind between Emerson and the Bible, with the difference that now
they no longer seem to conflict and she has at last made her peace with them
both:

To Mrs. J. C. Holland   after Christmas 1882

Sweet Sister.

The lovely recollection—the thought of those that cannot "taste"—of
one to whose faint Bed all Boons were brought before revealed, made the
sweet Package mighty—It came so long it knows the way and almost
comes itself, like Nature's faithful Blossoms whom no one summons but
themselves, Magics of Constancy—
The Fiction of "Santa Claus" always reminds me of the reply to my
early question of "Who made the Bible"—"Holy Men moved by the
Holy Ghost," and though I have now ceased my investigations, the
Solution is insufficient—
Santa Claus, though, *illustrates*—Revelation
But a Book is only the Heart's Portrait—every Page a Pulse—
Thank you for the protecting words—The petit Shepherd would find
us but a startled Flock, not an unloving one—
Remember me to your Possessions, in whom I have a tender claim,
and take sweet care of the small Life, fervor has made great—deathless
as Emerson's "Squirrel"—
Vinnie gives her love and will write, if a Lady goes away who is calling
here—Maggie prized your remembrance—Austin seldom calls—I am glad
you were glad to see him—He visits rarely as Gabriel—

                                              Lovingly,
                                                    Emily

The last words she put to paper compress the themes of a lifetime and
suggest that the valor and the ability to love that had enabled her to live with
doubt and to grow did not leave her at the end:

To Higginson, who was ill
                                              early May 1886

    Deity—does He live now?
    My friend—does he breathe?

To her Norcross Cousins
                                              May 1886

    Little Cousins,
        Called back.
        Emily.

Dickinson has often been thought of as deprived and weakened by the
narrowness of Amherst culture, by the emotional ties that bound her so closely
to her family and her home, by the inner necessities that confined her first to

house and garden and finally to her room. There is a sense in which it is quite true that she *was* deprived—of personal contact with other artists of comparable stature, even of contact with minds equal to hers and concerned with the same problems. Except in her reading, she was isolated from the best thought and the best minds of the time. None of her correspondents was capable of meeting her on her own intellectual level. But it has not often been seen how she managed to turn her deprivation into a source of strength.

I suspect we ought to think of the obtuseness and conventionalism that kept Higginson from recognizing the quality of her work as fortunate, for if he had been able to understand her and help her to get published, she might have been drawn to his kind of vapid idealism and bland moralism. As it was, she had no temptation to write in any way other than to please herself and her ideal reader. Higginson was incapable of corrupting her by drawing her out of her isolation into his own world of borrowed feelings and second-rate ideas.

When, after her death, he had been reluctantly persuaded to edit some of her poems for publication, first-rate minds immediately began to recognize her for one of themselves. The comment Alice James entered in her *Diary* upon reading the poems shortly after their publication is very much to the point:

> It is reassuring to hear the English pronouncement that Emily Dickinson is fifth-rate, they have such a capacity for missing quality; the robust evades them equally with the subtle. Her being sicklied o'er with T. W. Higginson makes one quake lest there be a latent flaw which escapes one's vision—but what tomes of philosophy *resumes* the cheap farce or expresses the highest point of view of the aspiring soul more completely than the following—

> > How dreary to be somebody
> > How public, like a frog
> > To tell your name the livelong day
> > To an admiring bog!

Dickinson at times would have liked to endure for a while the dreariness of being "somebody," but she found no way of reaching the "admiring bog"—for even Higginson, though his mind was sufficiently boggy, was not *admiring*. Failure, then, partly endured, partly sought, condemned her to be what she was and make do with what she had. What she had culturally was a uniquely fortunate dual heritage that condensed for her the poetic and spiritual resources of past and present and that, by eliminating the peripheral and the merely timely, kept her work in the main stream of the great tradition in American poetry. If one were forced to choose just one poet to illuminate the nature and quality of American poetry as a whole, to define its continuing pre-occupations, its characteristic themes and images—even to suggest the kinds of subjects and concerns typically *absent* in it—one ought to choose Dickinson.

There are very few important American poets either before or after her whose work is not suggested somewhere in hers, whose images she did not try out, whose insights she did not recapitulate, criticize, or anticipate. She not only bridged the gap between Edward Taylor and Emerson, she bridged the one between Emerson and Frost—and even, more rarely but distinctly enough—between Emerson and Eliot and Stevens. All this came as her special sensibility responded to her limited experience, and responded chiefly in terms of the Bible, Shakespeare, and Emerson. She would have been poorer without Shakespeare, but the Bible and Emerson, their conflict and their coherence, were what chiefly shaped her ideas, her language, her sensibility, and even her choice of verse forms.

The "common meter" which is the basis for almost all her work she adopted from the hymns she was hearing in "meeting" every Sunday. That the meter and stanzaic form of most of the older hymns was the same as that of the traditional folk ballads and the commonest nursery rhymes was a positive advantage from the Emersonian point of view that was hers by the time she reached poetic maturity. To write in this simplest and most "natural" of forms, the form chosen by Samuel Johnson when he extemporized a quatrain to illustrate for Boswell his idea that the mere presence of *verse* does not guarantee the presence of *poetry*—

> I put my hat upon my head
> And walked into the Strand,
> And there I met another man
> Whose hat was in his hand—

to write in *this* form would ensure that, whatever her verse might be like, it would not be that mere "tinkling of piano strings" that Emerson had condemned. In *this* form she would have to *say* something, or the result would be nothing at all.

Her earliest poem, apart from the sampler, is her verse Valentine of 1850. It begins like this:

> Awake ye muses nine, sing me a strain divine,
> Unwind the solemn twine, and tie my Valentine!

If she had only gone on like this, Higginson would have realized that she was writing poetry. But the voice is not her own. Conventional prosody and conventional language are being used for humorous effect. For serious poetry, for poetry that could convey "the noiseless noise in the garden" that she listened for and wanted to make others hear, for the *news* conveyed in her "letter to the world," she would have to find a form of her own, as Emerson had said so emphatically and repeatedly. If she wanted to be a "true poet," and not just a person "of poetical talents, or of industry and skill in metre," he had said, she would have to find a way of making the "argument" create the "metre." (The rest of the valentine is in "fourteeners.")

It was no accident that she turned to the form preferred by writers of hymns and ballads and nursery rhymes—a form debased in our time to being used in advertising jingles. It was a children's form—and she thought of herself increasingly, after she was twenty, as a little girl—or sometimes as a little boy, a little tippler, or even a little gnome. It had the great advantage of not being a "literary" form—though Wigglesworth had used it, and Bryant occasionally, and Emerson often. It suggested to her not literature but life her own, for in it the most important things had been said. She had perhaps heard sung a hymn new in her youth but written in the old form:

> There is a green hill far away
> Without a city wall,
> Where our dear Lord was crucified
> Who died to save us all.

But whether she had heard this one or not does not matter, for Watt's *Christian Psalmnody* and his *Psalms, Hymns, and Spiritual Songs,* both part of her father's library, were full of both this meter, and its variations, and this *thought,* and *its* variations. If now in the first flush of her revolt against her father's religion she chose to deny the thought, how better deny it than in the form in which the thought was most commonly expressed, a real poetic form that would not seem to be a form at all but simply *a vehicle* for thought? The chief problem created by such a choice might be to keep the poems from sounding too much like

> Mary had a little lamb,
> Its fleece was white as snow,
> And everywhere that Mary went,
> The lamb was sure to go.

but that could be prevented by deliberate roughening of meter, by using slant rhymes or none, by breaking up the stanza, or by doing all three at once. This form and the variations of it—listed and named by Watts—not only provided the pattern for almost all of her early poems, but was used without need for any significant alteration in most of the greatest poems of her late maturity, such as "A Route of Evanescence," "A single Clover Plank," "The Road was lit with Moon and Star," "And with what body do they come?," "Glass was the Street—in tinsel Peril," "My life closed twice before its close," and many others.

The advantage the form had for her of which she was *conscious* is made clear in a poem a part of which I have already quoted in a connection having nothing to do with form, but the poem is short enough, and interesting enough, to bear partial repetition:

> The murmuring of Bees, has ceased
> But murmuring of some
> Posterior, prophetic,

Has simultaneous come.
The lower metres of the Year
When Nature's laugh is done
The Revelations of the Book
Whose Genesis was June.
Appropriate Creatures to her change
The Typic Mother sends
As Accent fades to interval
With separating Friends
Till what we speculate, has been
And thoughts we will not show
More intimate with us become
Than Persons, that we know.

The poem is richer of course than a mere comment on form, on choice of "meters," but something about that choice is surely *one* of the things it is saying. "Lower" and more "natural" meters are appropriate to the time; when the murmuring of bees is heard no more in reality, it had better not be heard in too melodious verse. Here as so often she foreshadows both Frost and Stevens, particularly the former's "Oven Bird" and the latter's "Sad Strains of a Gay Waltz." Her meters were one of her strategies for dealing with a world she anticipated both of them in seeing as "diminished," as Frost would put it. As she had put it in an earlier poem, poets in her time had to learn to sing "a few prosaic days," after the bright autumnal colors were gone and before the snow came. How better to do this than in the commonest and plainest of forms?

One of her late poems will illustrate what she learned to do with a form associated chiefly in her mind with doggerel and jingles—how she created a new poetic intensity of suggestion in a form recommended to her chiefly by its prosaic, almost its anti-poetic, quality. There are no murmurings of bees in the following poem, dating from about 1872, but the "music" of idea that has found its form:

Like Rain it sounded till it curved
And then I knew 'twas Wind—
It walked as wet as any Wave
But swept as dry as sand—
When it had pushed itself away
To some remotest Plain
A coming as of Hosts was heard
That was indeed the Rain—
It filled the Wells, it pleased the Pools
It warbled in the Road—
It pulled the spigot from the Hills
And let the Floods abroad—
It loosened acres, lifted seas

> The sites of Centres stirred
> Then like Elijah rode away
> Upon a Wheel of Cloud.

The Bible and Emerson unite here, the Bible supplying imagery that is finally interpreted in Emersonian terms that alter but do not cancel the Biblical meanings. Is it then a Biblical poem or a Transcendental one? The answer of course is that it is both and neither. It springs from an amalgamation of her two heritages that by this time was peculiarly her own.

The Biblical sources are I Kings, Chapters 17 and 18; II Kings, 2:1; II Kings, 2:11 and Ezekiel, Chapter 1. The passages in first and second Kings tell of Elijah, who recalled his people to the worship of the true God. Behind the poem is the drought recorded in I Kings, sent by the Lord to punish the Israelites for their apostasy. During the course of the drought, Elijah performed a miracle of resurrection:

> And he stretched himself unto the child three times, and cried unto the Lord, and said, O Lord my God, I pray thee, let this child's soul come into him again.
> And the Lord heard the voice of Elijah; and the soul of the child came into him again, and he revived. (I Kings, 17:21-22.)

Having asked the people how long they would "halt . . . between two opinions" and having mocked them for worshipping Baal, Elijah rebuilt the broken altar, "and it came to pass . . . that the heaven was black with clouds and wind, and there was a great rain" (I Kings, 18:45). Second Kings provides the image of a "whirlwind," and of a "chariot of fire," in which the Lord carried Elijah up into heaven—the image utilized in the last two lines of the poem. But the vision of God in the first chapter of Ezekiel is perhaps the most crucial of the three Biblical sources. Here again we have a whirlwind, but this time it does not carry the prophet away, but brings him a vision: "out of the midst thereof came the likeness of four living creatures. And this was their appearance; they had the likeness of a man."

These creatures of dream with their multiple faces and wings but their "likeness of a man" appeared to be carried in, or perhaps to be synonymous with, a mystic vehicle composed of nothing but wheels: "and their appearance and their work was as it were a wheel in the middle of a wheel"; "for the spirit of the living creatures was in the wheels."

> And when they went, I heard the noise of their wings, like the noise of great waters, as the voice of the Almighty, as the voice of speech, as the noise of an host. . . .
> And above the firmament . . . was the likeness of a throne. . . . and upon the throne was the likeness as the appearance of a man. . . .
> As the appearance of the bow that is in the cloud in the day of rain, so was the appearance of the brightness round about. This was the

appearance of the likeness of the glory of the Lord. And when I saw it, I fell upon my face, and I heard a voice of one that spake.

And he said unto me, Son of man, stand upon thy feet, and I will speak unto thee.

(Ezekiel 1:24-28, 2:1)

This vision of Ezekiel's has often been interpreted, as it was by Blake, as a vision of man lifted up into god-likeness. If this is the way Dickinson read it, as I suspect, then the Lord's command, stand upon thy feet, conforms exactly to Emerson's advice and is a part of the meaning of the poem. And the Biblical *image* also matches Emerson's image of spiritual growth; for in "Circles" he had written that only "the force of the individual soul" determined "the extent to which this generation of circles, wheel without wheel," could go. Just two final notes and I shall leave the matter of sources. The sea in Dickinson's poems is almost always, and certainly here, death, which would make "lifted" seas consistent with the resurrection imagery of the Biblical sources (Revelation, 21:1, 4: "a new heaven and a new earth . . . no more sea . . . no more death."); and the "Centres" whose sites are stirred should be interpreted, I think, as an allusion to that definition of God that Dickinson had got from Emerson—as a being whose center was everywhere and circumference nowhere.

If we recall how Emerson had defined reality as "a system of concentric circles," and how often Dickinson used the image of the wheel to suggest what she called, with Emerson, circumference, we may perhaps interpret the "Wheel of Cloud" as the ultimate of circumference. But whatever the poem "means," it is clear that it could not have been written at all if either part of the poet's heritage had been missing. It might be described as a Biblical poem containing its own Emersonian gloss.

If, by concentrating so exclusively on Emerson and the Bible as essential to the special quality and special achievement of her work, I have by this time created the impression that Emerson and the Bible were all she knew, that impression was far from intended. She read constantly and penetratingly. Forgetting about her art for the moment, we may say that the quality of her *thought* alone would put this somewhat hysterical woman in a class with the best minds of her age.

Take her criticisms of Biblical faith, for example. While a great many quite thoughtful people were worrying about the conflict between Darwin's theory of evolution and the account of creation given in *Genesis,* interpreted as literal history, she simply ignored this whole "problem." She could have written just as she did if Darwin had not published *Origin of Species* in the very year, 1859, when her great productive period began. Darwin offered no shock to one who had absorbed his Emerson as well as she had.

Or take her criticisms of Emerson. Apart from differences of temperament and situation which made her say of the master in effect just what Melville scribbled in the margin of one of Emerson's essays, that this man must never have experienced a toothache, her criticism of the philosophy considered as a substitute for her father's religion anticipated by a quarter of a century the criticism that William James would make in *The Varieties of Religious Experience*. When, in his "Conclusion," James turned from his discussion of what seemed to him, speaking as a scientist and philosopher, *verifiable* statements about religious experience, and began, brave spirit that he was, to offer his own "over-beliefs"—that is, beliefs beyond the evidence, as it had finally seemed to Dickinson and it continued to seem to him religious belief must always be—he told his audience why, despite his inability to accept any religious orthodoxy, he preferred to continue to use the word "God" rather than to follow Emerson's example and say something like "Oversoul" or "eternal generator of circles." "God," he wrote,

> is the natural appellation, for us Christians at least, for the supreme reality, so I will call this higher part of the universe by the name of God. . . . [In doing so, he said he was only following] the instinctive belief of mankind: God is real since he produces real effects. [Then, as a footnote to the first of these sentences, he added:] Transcendentalists are fond of the term "Over-soul," but as a rule they use it in an intellectualist sense, as meaning only a medium of communion. "God" is a causal agent as well as a medium of communion, and that is the aspect which I wish to emphasize. [Then, in the "Postscript," footnoting the sentence, "Both instinctively and for logical reasons, I find it hard to believe that principles can exist which make no difference in facts," he thinks again of Transcendentalism as his best example:]

> Transcendental idealism, of course, insists that its ideal world makes *this* difference, that facts *exist*. We owe it to the Absolute that we have a world of fact at all. 'A world' of fact!—that exactly is the trouble. An entire world is the smallest unit with which the Absolute can work, whereas to our finite minds work for the better ought to be done within this world, setting in at single points. Our difficulties and our ideals are all piecemeal affairs, but the Absolute can do no piecework for us; so that all the interests which our poor souls compass raise their heads too late. We should have spoken earlier, prayed for another world absolutely, before this world was born. It is strange, I have heard a friend say, to see this blind corner into which Christian thought has worked itself at last, with its God who can raise no particular weight whatever, who can help us with no private burden, and who is on the side of our enemies as much as he is on our own. Odd evolution from the God of David's psalms!

There is also a very close parallel between the poet's thoughts and the scientist-philosopher's on what might be meant if one called the self "transcendent," as he did, or simply assumed transcendence without using the word, as she did. James might be paraphrasing a dozen Dickinson poems when, in his "Conclusion" to *Varieties,* he first states his conviction, then adds his "over-belief" on the dimensions of the self:

> The reason [why the "scientific attitude" is "shallow" when used to explain away religion] is that, so long as we deal with the cosmic and

the general we deal only with the symbols of reality, but *as soon as we deal with private and personal phenomena as such, we deal with realities in the completest sense of the term.* [Italics James's. And now the over-belief.] The further limits of our being plunge, it seems to me, into an altogether other dimension of existence from the sensible and merely "understandable" world. Name it the mystical region, or the supernatural region, whichever you choose.

Since the James family has been drawn upon so often already in this discussion, in my effort to counter the currently prominent, and I fear growing, notion that Dickinson ought to be thought of either as a quaint provincial, or as a compulsive neurotic, in her thinking about time and death and religious faith as required by belief in the transcendence of the self, no one will be surprised if I cite as a last example of the sophistication of the thinking of this secluded and tortured woman a comment by Henry James the novelist on the question of "Immortality," a word that occupies so prominent a place in all her poetry.

Over and over in her last years, we recall, Dickinson had said that the *evidence* available to her, lacking as she did any such mystical experience as Whitman had had, was insufficient to support any definite religious belief on the subject at all, so that all she had to go on was her "uncertain certainty," her "guess" or "surmise," and her willed commitment to the Possible. As she said in one poem, "Of Death I try to think like this." To "try" to think is to be aware of the whole extent of the problem.

In the conclusion of the essay "Is There a Life After Death?" which he contributed in 1910 to a volume called *In After Days, Thoughts on the Future Life,* James, who was no more a philosopher than she, not only reached something very like her conclusion but reached it by a similar route. The poet's *trying* to think he put as *liking* to think, a change of wording which, in the context of such a discussion, amounted to no change at all in attitude and assumption. We cannot know, he wrote, how we *ought* to think about such matters, but

> If I am talking, at all events, of what I "like" to think, I may, in short, say all: I like to think it open to me to establish speculative and imaginative connections, to take up conceived presumptions and pledges, that have for me all the air of not being decently able to escape redeeming themselves. And when once such a mental relation to the question as that begins to hover and settle, who shall say over what fields of experience, past and current, and what immensities of perception and yearning, it shall *not* spread the protection of its wings? No, no, no—I reach beyond the laboratory-brain.

. . . The point is that Dickinson had thought the same way thirty years earlier.

From "Emily Dickinson: The Transcendent Self," *Criticism,* 7 (1965), 297-334.

JOHN PICKARD

Achievement

AMONG OUTSTANDING American writers few had to wait as long for critical and scholarly acceptance as did Emily Dickinson. With just seven poems published in her lifetime, it was not until the 1950s that she was securely placed with Poe and Whitman as a major poet. Such posthumous fame fitted the anonymity of her life and echoed her own prophecy to Higginson: "If fame belonged to me, I could not escape her—if she did not, the longest day would pass me on the chase." Perhaps her unschooled "Barefoot-Rank" better suited her solitary existence than any contemporary fame. Certainly, she carefully maneuvered her withdrawal from Amherst society and tenaciously fought for privacy throughout her life.

Although Transcendentalism's concept of self-reliance satisfied her inquiring spirit more than Calvinism's harsh dogmas, her mind displayed the essential religious texture of the Puritan mentality. Lacking the orthodox confidence in salvation, she employed Puritanism's belief in self-denial to rein her passionate, sensitive nature. Her own suffering taught her that pain and deprivation, rather than happiness, constituted the essence of life. She eschewed the conventional supports of home, society, and religion to fight alone on life's hardest battle-ground—within the human soul. Unflinchingly she faced inner challenges and struggled to wrest spiritual victory from emotional defeat. Basically she was a religious poet whose concern with the fundamental issues of death, pain, love, and immortality occasioned her finest lyrics. She revitalized the usual poetic approach to God and religion and in her scrupulous record of the soul's "Adventure ...unto itself" explored new frontiers of sensations and psychological experience. Neither a consistent nor original thinker, she pragmatically tested traditional concepts before accepting their validity. Always analyzing, she sought to tell "all the Truth" and to stun her hearers with the resulting "Bolts of Melody." Like many poets she perceived man as a beleaguered, isolated creature, desperately seeking truth in a relativistic world. Mainly her own thwarted love, unfulfilled poetic ambitions, and dissatisfaction with Calvinism furnished the crude clay from which she molded her finished poems. From her limited, pain-filled experiences she wrung an intense exhilaration with the processes of life. In her poetry she expressed these feelings so originally that the provincial and the private were often translated into enduring, universal art.

Her poetic strategy depended upon the "language of surprise," wit, paradox, and irony, to reveal the naked soul in dramatic conflict with established conventions. Though fascinated by words, she ruthlessly omitted phrases and cut through syntax to achieve conciseness and to capture the spontaneity and excitement of her thoughts. If at times her economy short-circuited full meaning, it also infused her poetry with an electric vibrancy that rivaled the intimacy of the spoken word. As her subjects were limited, so her stylistic traits, aside from her eccentric punctuation, were mainly conventional: hymnal stanzas, repetitive iambics, and a fondness for colloquial expressions and approximate rhyme. Still, her imaginative sense and profound artistic dedication transformed these familiar devices into a lively medium for her thoughts. Of course, critics have extensively catalogued her glaring failures: rampant sentimentality, an excessive preoccupation with death and pain, awkward inversions, monotonous metrics, and an over-all inability to control her exploding poetic force. Yet, measured against the vitality and imaginative scope of her verses, these objections become mere cavils. One gauge of her achievement was the popular appreciation of her poetry long before academicians considered her verse acceptable. Only Robert Frost has had a similar popular and critical success.

Undoubtedly, the areas of life and nature that most interested her were narrow and personal. Still, she probed these subjects deeply and produced a surprising variety of insights about external nature, the inner struggles of the human soul, and the mysteries of death and immortality. Though her nature poems often deal with the pictorial aspects of flowers and sunsets, her most original ones, like "A Route of Evanescence," touch upon the strangeness and elusiveness of nature's "haunted house." "These are the days when Birds come back" and "A Light exists in Spring" imbue the material scene with distinctive religious and regal imagery to sound philosophic overtones. Repeatedly she observed the change of seasons and moments of storm and chose nature's odd creatures to enliven the conventional romantic view of nature. "Of Bronze— and Blaze" utilizes the solemn grandeur of the universe to evoke hauntingly man's frail mortality, while "Further in Summer than the Birds" employs the pensive rituals of a dying year to demonstrate man's alienation from nature.

Another major poetic grouping records an overwhelming passion that progresses to a climatic meeting of the lovers, only to collapse into despairing separation. Even the tensions of physical attraction were frankly handled in poems like "My Life had stood—a Loaded Gun," while another group of poems longingly surveys a wife's estate in marriage. The anxiety of denial and loss provided the framework for intense psychological analyses that gradually brought spiritual consolation. Her sublimation of passion into a religious triumph originated some of her most moving love lyrics, for example, "Title divine—is mine" and "Mine—by the Right of White Election." Continually her poems affirm the value of renunciation, minutely scrutinizing the spiritual good that emerged from such rejection. Like Hawthorne she praised heroism in defeat and carefully examined the educative nature of pain. Many poems commend the stoic courage of those who silently endure their "Calvary of

Wo." "Renunciation—is a piercing Virtue" analyzes both the poignancy and bitterness of denial, and "After great pain, a formal feeling comes" portrays the soul's numbed response to an enervating shock.

However, her most searching explorations within the human spirit dealt with death and immortality. She portrayed death from every possible aspect: as the courtly lover, the dreadful assassin, the physical corrupter, and the one free agent in nature. For her, death remained the supreme experience, which brought either new spiritual existence or lifeless immobility. "Because I could not stop for Death," "I Heard a Fly buzz—when I died," and "A Clock stopped" view death's inexorable power, highlighting the physical transformation and chilling isolation that it causes. Often she contrasted the pious expectations of death with its grim reality, employing funereal and religious imagery to dramatize death's approach. Although she interchanged the terms "death" and "immortality," she usually envisioned death as the threshold of that new state. The "Flood subject" of immortality both baffled and intrigued her, and the resulting tensions produced "Behind Me—dips Eternity" and "Safe in their Alabaster Chambers." Though one later poem, "Those not live yet," triumphantly asserts that death brings no change to the immortal soul, she never ceased questioning or anatomizing those ultimates. Reading through her collected poems, one is startled afresh by man's infinite capacity to endure and master suffering.

She once expressed the extent of her achievement:

> The Poets light but Lamps—
> Themselves—go out—
> The Wicks they stimulate—
> If vital Light
>
> Inhere as do the Suns—
> . . . .
> Disseminating their
> Circumference—

Certainly the vital light of genius illuminates her poems. With each succeeding generation they have shone brighter, disseminating their radiant vision of circumference with increasing power and beauty.

From *Emily Dickinson: An Introduction and Interpretation* (New York: Holt, Rinehart and Winston, 1967), pp. 122-25.

CHARLES ANDERSON

Conclusion

THE FINAL direction of her poetry, and the pressures that created it, can only be described as religious, using that word in its 'dimension of depth.' As defined by one of the truly creative theologians of the twentieth century, Paul Tillich, this differs widely from what is conventionally understood by the term: it means 'asking passionately the question of the meaning of our existence, . . . and of *being* universally, . . . even if the answers hurt.' It is not necessarily connected with the creeds and activities of particular institutions dedicated to belief in the existence of God and devotion to His service. Indeed, many people who have been grasped by this infinite concern feel themselves far removed from historical religion because of its inadequacy in expressing their concern: 'They are religious while rejecting the religions.' Loss of the dimension of depth in religion, Tillich feels, is the result of modern man's estrangement from his world and from his self. As a consequence, the great religious symbols by which this concern has been expressed in Western civilization have lost their power. It is notable that this religious thinker concludes by finding painters and poets are the most sharply aware of the human predicament today—as revealed in their themes, their styles, their imagery—the ones most passionately searching to recover this lost dimension by revitalizing the traditional symbols or creating new ones that fit the particular modern dilemma. This is precisely the purpose of Dickinson's explorations of the self and external nature in her poetry, often beginning with Biblical language and metaphor, then transmuting these into new forms through the creative power of words, to render her experience of what it means to be human.

Another representative philosopher of our times, A. N. Whitehead, in describing the decay of religious values under the impact of science, fills out this area of relevance in her poetry for readers today. Religion will never regain its old power, he feels, until it can face change in the same spirit as science does. Noting that no belief can be contained permanently in the same mold, he emphasizes the need to "preserve the life in a flux of form," especially in an age when religion is degenerating into a mere formula to embellish a complacent society. Though Whitehead's own attempt at redefinition is offered diffidently, it has real pertinence to the present inquiry. "Religion is the reaction of human nature to its search for God," he says, and since this is chiefly manifested as worship, "The worship of God . . . is an adventure of the spirit, a flight after the unattainable." Then more fully:

Religion is the vision of something which stands beyond, behind, and within, the passing flux of immediate things; something which is real, and yet waiting to be realized; something which is a remote possibility, and yet the greatest of present facts; something that gives meaning to all that passes, and yet eludes apprehension; something whose possession is the final good, and yet is beyond all reach; something which is the ultimate ideal, and the hopeless quest.

The most effective formulations of this quest, he also concludes, will come from the imagination of the artist rather than from philosophical or theological thought. And it is notable how closely his own definitions fit the creative vision Emily Dickinson tried to fix in her poetry. These modern analogies should make clear what is meant by the claim that she is a religious poet.

Her great talents, to be sure, are those of a highly original sayer, not a seer. To set this emphasis right one more analogy will be cited in conclusion, the literary one used at the beginning of this book. If significance in literature can be measured by the quantity of metaphor thrown up, as Henry James believed, then her poems on death and immortality represent the summit of her achievement. The novelty and brilliance of her imagery in these last two chapters are memorable. Within the context of the individual poems, old and new symbols are maneuvered by the language of surprise so as to illuminate the two profoundest themes that challenged her poetic powers. This reveals her kinship with another article of James' esthetic faith: if the creative writer pushes far enough into language he finds himself in the embrace of thought. By slant and surprise, by wit and a novel reworking of traditional modes, she evolved a way with words that became her instrument of knowing. Committed to nothing but dedicated to a search for truth and beauty, hers was a free spirit for whom living was a succession of intense experiences and art an endless exploration of their meanings. A poet rather than a systematic thinker, she never came up with dogmatic answers. Indeed her most effective verbal strategy was to exploit ambiguity, as in the conflicting attitudes towards her flood subject Immortality.

In her personal life, as well as in her poetry, alternating doubt and belief held her mind unresolved to the very end. Her next to last letter, according to the dating by her editors, was a brief note to Higginson: "Deity—does He live now? My friend—does he breathe?" The very last letter she ever wrote, addressed to her Norcross cousins just before her death on May 15, 1886, was also her shortest: "Called back.' And the smallest bit of manuscript that has come down, measuring one half by one and a half inches, records in her latest handwriting: "Grasped by God." The true ordering of these undated jottings can probably never be known, nor what her last words were on this mighty theme. But this is of no importance here. Her personal faith and the final destiny of her soul lie outside the bounds of a book concerned exclusively with her creative achievement. The tensions that created the great poems had been relaxed. In them, at least, she gained some measure of immortality. . . .

From *Emily Dickinson's Poetry: Stairway of Surprise* (New York: Holt, Rinehart and Winston, 1960), pp. 283-85.

ADRIENNE RICH

"E."

'Halfcracked' to Higginson, living,
afterward famous in garbled versions—
your hoard of dazzling scraps a battlefield—
now your old snood

mothballed at Harvard
and you in your variorum monument
equivocal to the end—
who are you?

Gardening the day-lily,
wiping the wine-glass stems,
your thought pulsed on behind
a forehead battered paper-thin,

you, woman, masculine
in singlemindedness,
for whom the word was more
than a symptom—

a condition of being.
Till the air buzzing with spoiled language
sang in your ears
of Perjury

and in your halfcracked way you chose
silence for entertainment,
chose to have it out at last
on your own premises.

From Albert Gelpi, *Emily Dickinson: The Mind of the Poet* (Cambridge: Harvard Univ. Press, 1965), p. xiii.

SELECTED BIBLIOGRAPHY

Editions of Emily Dickinson's Poems

Poems by Emily Dickinson. Ed. Mabel Loomis Todd and T. W. Higginson. Boston: Roberts Brothers, 1890.

Poems by Emily Dickinson, Second Series. Ed. T. W. Higginson and Mabel Loomis Todd. Boston: Roberts Brothers, 1891.

Poems by Emily Dickinson, Third Series. Ed. Mabel Loomis Todd. Boston: Roberts Brothers, 1896.

The Single Hound. Ed. Martha Dickinson Bianchi. Boston: Little, Brown, 1914.

Further Poems of Emily Dickinson Withheld from Publication by Her Sister Lavinia. Ed. Martha Dickinson Bianchi and Alfred Leete Hampson. Boston: Little, Brown, 1929.

The Poems of Emily Dickinson. Ed. Martha Dickinson Bianchi and Alfred Leete Hampson. Boston: Little, Brown, 1937.

Bolts of Melody. Ed. Mabel Loomis Todd and Millicent Todd Bingham. New York: Harper & Row, 1945.

The Poems of Emily Dickinson, Including Variant Readings Critically Compared with All Known Manuscripts. Ed. Thomas H. Johnson. 3 vols. Cambridge: Harvard Univ. Press, 1955. Upon this definitive edition all subsequent scholarship rests.

The Complete Poems of Emily Dickinson. Ed. Thomas H. Johnson. Boston: Little, Brown, 1960. A one-volume edition, without the variant versions; organized chronologically.

Final Harvest: Emily Dickinson's Poems. Ed. Thomas H. Johnson. Boston: Little, Brown, 1962. A selection of 575 poems from the variorum edition of 1955.

Letters

Letters of Emily Dickinson. Ed. Mabel Loomis Todd. 2 vols. Boston: Roberts Brothers, 1894.

Letters of Emily Dickinson. Ed. Mabel Loomis Todd. New York: Harper & Row, 1931.

Emily Dickinson: A Revelation. Ed. Millicent Todd Bingham. New York: Harper & Row, 1954.

The Letters of Emily Dickinson, Ed. Thomas H. Johnson. 3 vols. Cambridge: Harvard Univ. Press, 1958. The definitive edition.

Bibliography

Clendenning, Sheila T. *Emily Dickinson: A Bibliography. 1850-1966.* Kent, Ohio: Kent State Univ. Press, 1968.

Rosenbaum, S. P., Ed. *A Concordance to the Poems of Emily Dickinson.* Ithaca, N.Y.: Cornell Univ. Press, 1964.

Spiller, Robert E. et al. *Literary History of the United States: Bibliography.* 3rd ed. rev. New York: Macmillan, 1963.

Woodress, James L. *American Literary Scholarship: An Annual, 1963.* Durham, N.C.: Duke Univ. Press, 1964.

Biography

Bianchi, Martha Dickinson. *The Life and Letters of Emily Dickinson*. Boston: Houghton Mifflin, 1924.

Bianchi, Martha Dickinson. *Emily Dickinson Face to Face*. Boston: Houghton Mifflin, 1932.

Bingham, Millicent Todd. *Ancestor's Brocades: The Literary Debut of Emily Dickinson*. New York: Harper & Row, 1945.

Jackson, Helen Hunt. *Mercy Philbrick's Choice*. Boston: Roberts Brothers, 1876. A popular novel based on her life by one who knew her.

Johnson, Thomas H. *Emily Dickinson: An Interpretive Biography*. Cambridge: The Belknap Press of Harvard Univ. Press, 1955.

Leyda, Jay. *The Years and Hours of Emily Dickinson*. 2 vols. New Haven: Yale Univ. Press, 1960. A log book of public and private records; a collection of sources rather than a discursive biography. Quite valuable.

Patterson, Rebecca. *The Riddle of Emily Dickinson*. Boston: Houghton Mifflin, 1951. The riddle is a broken love affair with Kate Anthon.

Pollit, Josephine. *Emily Dickinson: The Human Background of Her Poetry*. New York: Harper & Row, 1930.

Taggard, Genevieve. *The Life and Mind of Emily Dickinson*. New York: Knopf, 1930.

Ward, Theodora. *The Capsule of the Mind: Chapters in the Life of Emily Dickinson*. Cambridge: Harvard Univ. Press, 1961.

Whicher, George Frisbie. *This Was A Poet*. New York: Charles Scribner's Sons, 1938.

Critical Studies

Anderson, Charles. *Emily Dickinson's Poetry: Stairway of Surprise*. New York: Holt, Rinehart, and Winston, 1960. The first complete critical study.

Bogan, Louise, Archibald MacLeish, and Richard Wilbur. *Emily Dickinson: Three Views*. Amherst: Amherst College Press, 1960. A symposium at Amherst; Miss Bogan's paper is entitled "A Mystical Poet"; Mr. MacLeish's, "The Private World," and Mr. Wilbur's, "Sumptuous Destitution."

Blake, Caesar Robert and Carlton F. Wells, Ed. *The Recognition of Emily Dickinson, Selected Criticism Since 1890*. Ann Arbor: Univ. of Michigan Press, 1964. A valuable collection of diverse critical interpretations.

Capps, Jack L. *Emily Dickinson's Reading, 1836-1886*. Cambridge: Harvard Univ. Press, 1966.

Chase, Richard V. *Emily Dickinson*. New York: William Sloane, 1951.

Davis, Thomas M. *Fourteen by Emily Dickinson: With Selected Criticism*. Fair Lawn, N.J.: Scott, Foresman, 1964. Fourteen of her best poems, each followed by several critical analyses and evaluations. Useful.

Gelpi, Albert J. *Emily Dickinson: The Mind of the Poet*. Cambridge: Harvard Univ. Pres, 1965.

Griffith, Clark. *The Long Shadow: Emily Dickinson's Tragic Poetry*. Princeton: Princeton Univ. Press, 1964.

Higgins, David J. M. *Portrait of Emily Dickinson: The Poet and Her Prose*. New Brunswick, N.J.: Rutgers Univ. Press, 1967. Demonstrates the importance of her letters and their relation to her poetry. Identifies "Master" as Samuel Bowles.

Longworth, Polly. *Emily Dickinson: Her Letter to the World*. New York: Crowell, 1965.

Lubbers, Klaus. *Emily Dickinson: The Critical Revolution*. Ann Arbor: Univ. of Michigan Press, 1968.

Miller, Ruth. *The Poetry of Emily Dickinson.* Middletown, Conn.: Wesleyan Univ. Press, 1968.

Pearce, Roy Harvey. *The Continuity of American Poetry.* Princeton: Princeton Univ. Press, 1961. Perhaps the most valuable single study of American poetry as a whole. Strongly recommended.

Pickard, John. *Emily Dickinson: An Introduction and Interpretation.* New York: Holt, Rinehart, and Winston, 1967. A volume in the useful American Authors and Critics Series.

Porter, David. *The Art of Emily Dickinson's Early Poetry.* Cambridge: Harvard Univ. Press, 1966.

Sewell, Richard B., Ed. *Emily Dickinson: A Collection of Critical Essays.* Englewood Cliffs: Prentice-Hall, 1963.

Seyersted, Brita Lindberg. *The Voice of the Poet: Aspects Of Style in the Poetry of Emily Dickinson.* Cambridge: Harvard Univ. Press, 1968.

Sherwood, William R. *Circumference and Circumstance: Stages in the Mind and Art of Emily Dickinson.* New York: Columbia Univ. Press, 1968.

Wells, Henry W. *Introduction to Emily Dickinson.* Chicago: Packard, 1947.

Critical Articles

Adams, Richard P. "Dickinson Concrete." *Emerson Society Quarterly,* 44 (1966), 31-35.

Aldrich, Thomas Bailey. *"In Re* Emily Dickinson." *Atlantic Monthly,* 69 (Jan 1892), 143-44. Aldrich represents the typical poetic taste of Emily Dickinson's day.

Arvin, Newton. "The Poems of Emily Dickinson." *American Literature,* 28 (1956), 232-36.

Blackmur, Richard P. "Emily Dickinson: Notes on Prejudice and Fact." *The Southern Review,* 3 (1937): rpt. *The Expense of Greatness.* New York: Harcourt, Brace, and World, 1952.

Brooks, Cleanth. and Robert Penn Warren. Analysis of "After great pain, a formal feeling comes." *Understanding Poetry.* New York: Henry Holt, 1938.

Lynen, John F. "Three Uses of the Present: The Historian's, The Critic's, and Emily Dickinson's." *College English,* 28 (1966), 126-36.

Matthiesson, F. O. "The Problem of the Private Poet." *Kenyon Review,* 7 (1945), 584-97.

Moore, Marianne. "Emily Dickinson." *Poetry,* 41 (January 1933), 219-26.

Patterson, Rebecca. "Emily Dickinson's Palette." *Midwest Quarterly,* 5 (1963), 271292;: 6 (1964), 98-117.

Sewell, Richard B. "Emily Dickinson: New Looks and Fresh Starts." *Modern Language Quarterly,* 29 (1968), 84-90.

Stamm, Edith Perry. "Emily Dickinson: Poetry and Punctuation." *The Saturday Review,* 30 March 1963, pp. 26-27, 74.

Waggoner, Hyatt H. "Emily Dickinson: The Transcendent Self." *Criticism,* 7 (1965), 297-334.

Warren, Austin. "Emily Dickinson." *Sewanee Review,* 65 (1957), 565-86.

Wilson, Suzanne W. "Emily Dickinson and Twentieth-Century Poetry of Sensibility." *American Literature,* 36 (1964), 349-58.

Wilson, Suzanne W. "Structured Patterns in the Poetry of Emily Dickinson." *American Literature,* 35 (1963), 53-59.

Winters, Yvor. "Emily Dickinson and the Limits of Judgment.,' *Maule's Curse.* Norfolk, Conn.: New Directions, 1938.

Wright, Nathalia. "Emily Dickinson's Boanerges and Thoreau's Atropos: Locomotives on the Same Line?" *Modern Language Notes,* 82 (1957), 101-103.